China—

The New Creative Power in Architecture

China—

Chris van Uffelen

The New Creative Power in Architecture

BRAUN

Studio | Project

14 — 21
Introduction
Chris van Uffelen *

22 — 27
Coordination Asia
Zhang Lin, Tilman Thürmer
Project: Rainbow Chapel
Project Location: Shanghai

28 — 33
Bao Wei Architecture Office
Wei Bao
Project: Rooftop House
Project Location: Beijing

34 — 39
LLLab.
Hanxiao Liu, Luís Ricardo, David Correa, Taichi Kuma
Project: San Sa Village
Project Location: Beigou Village

40 — 45
DnA_Design and Architecture
Xu Tiantian
Project: Dushan Leisure Center
Project Location: Lishui

* In Chinese, personal names state the surname first, followed by the given name. Because of the international scope of this publication and in accordance with recognized standards, all personal names are written in the western sequence, i.e. with the given name followed by the surname. Exceptions are marked by an red asterisk.

Studio | Project

46 — 51
People's Architecture Office
Zhe He, James Shen, Feng Zang
Project: Shangwei Village Plugin Houses
Project Location: Shenzhen

52 — 57
3andwich Design
Wei He, Long Chen
Project: Limestone Gallery
Project Location: Dushan

58 — 63
RooMoo Design
Hui Zhang, Rui Zhang, Tao Zhang, Marine Bois
Project: Canada Goose Shanghai Office
Project Location: Shanghai

64 — 69
Taolei Architectural Design
Tao Lei
Project: Own House of Architect
Project Location: Beijing

70 — 75
B.L.U.E. Architecture Studio
Shuhei Aoyama
Project: Ota Fine Arts Gallery
Project Location: Shanghai

76 — 81
Shing & Partners Design Group
Eric Shing
Project: The Landmark
Project Location: Guangzhou

Studio | Project

82 — 87
CLOU architects
Jan Clostermann, Zhi Zhang, Jianyun Wu, Lin Li, Weiming Li
Project: Vantone Center
Project Location: Hangzhou

88 — 93
Atelier Alter Architects
Xiaojun Bu, Yingfan Zhang
Project: BIT Sports Center
Project Location: Beijing

94 — 99
Crossboundaries
Binke Lenhardt, Hao Dong
Project: Beisha Village Kindergarten
Project Location: Beisha Village

100 — 105
Sò Studio
Yifan Wu, Mengjie Liu
Project: The Beast Taikoo Li Store
Project Location: Beijing

106 — 111
U10 Atelier CADG
Haiwei Yu
Project: Hulunbuir Hailar Airport Expansion
Project Location: Hulunbuir

112 — 117
CU Office
Fei Che, Xuefeng Zhang
Project: Villa Jian Art Museum
Project Location: Yantai

Studio	Project
118 –123 Superimpose Architecture Carolyn Leung, Ben de Lange, Ruben Bergambagt	Project: CO2 Pavilion Project Location: Beijing
124 – 129 HHDFUN Zhenfei Wang, Luming Wang	Project: Dichi Service Center Project Location: Qingdao
130 – 135 Scenic Architecture Office Xiaofeng Zhu	Project: Shanghai Google Creators' Society Center Project Location: Shanghai
136 – 141 MTMdesign Max Trullás, Fanghai	Project: Heritage by Madison Project Location: Shanghai
142 – 147 Atelier DYJG Qing Lin, Xiangrong Wang	Project: Quarry Gardens Project Location: Nanning
148 – 153 Luo Studio Luo Yujie	Project: Longfu Life Experience Center Project Location: Puyang

Studio | Project

154 — 159
Miao Design Studio
Pu Miao
Project: Visitor Center, Xingxi Park
Project Location: Kunshan

160 — 165
Group of Architects
Hao Lu
Project: Alila Wuzhen
Project Location: Wuzhen

166 — 171
Hallucinate Design Office
Wenliang Wang
Project: Midwest Inland Port Financial Town
Project Location: Xi'an

172 —177
Interval Architects
Yunduan Gu, Oscar Ko
Project: Tower of Bricks
Project Location: Hengshui

178 — 183
Temp
Howard Jiho Kim
Project: Ajia Teahouse
Project Location: Hangzhou

184 — 189
ZZHK Architects
Zhang Ke
Project: Ruyi Bridge
Project Location: Chengdu

190 — 195
Yuan Ye Architects
Ye Yuan
Project: Bozhou Gymnasium
Project Location: Bozhou

Studio	Project
196 — 201 Atelier XÜK Xu Zhang, Kenan Liu	Project: Lostvilla Qinyong Primary School Hotel Project Location: Ningbo
202 — 207 SWA Group René Bihan, Ye Luo, Jim Lee	Project: Poly Future City Project Location: Beijing
208 — 213 Neri&Hu Design and Research Office Lyndon Neri, Rossana Hu	Project: Number 31 Project Location: Shanghai
214 — 219 O&O Studio Eric Chan, Suzanne Li, Katt Chung Yap	Project: Atelier Intimo Flagship Project Location: Shanghai
220 — 225 aoe Larry Wen	Project: Courtyard NO.1 Project Location: Heze
226 — 231 Benjai Architecture Qiao Xuesong, Li Xiang	Project: Nanjing Injoy Plaza Project Location: Nanjing
232 — 237 RhineScheme Lei Yang, Ran Li, Wolf Loebel	Project: IPPH-Headquarters Project Location: Beijing

Studio | Project

238 –243

Continuation Studio

Jiujiang Fan

Project: The Terraced House
Project Location: Dinghai

244 – 249

March Design

Wang Tao

Project: Wang Tao House
Project Location: Dali

250 – 255

Challenge Design

Jie Li

Project: Langtin Yuanzhu Experience Hall
Project Location: Wuhan

256– 261

AT Design

Mo Shen

Project: Laiyee Hostel
Project Location: Huzhou

262 – 267

ZJJZ

Sean Shen, Yu-Ying Tsai, Xuanru Chen

Project: Dafa Canal Tourist Information Center
Project Location: Zunyi

268 – 273

MenJue Architects

Manjun Huang, Tingting He, Fei Liu

Project: Shadow of Space Baishuiquan Tea House
Project Location: Shanghai

274 – 279

Zhang Hua Studio

Hua Zhang

Project: Yu Qingcheng Gallery
Project Location: Tianjin

Studio | Project

280 — 285
Atelier L+
Linxue Li
Project: Yellow River Ecological Tourist Wharf
Project Location: Dongying

286 — 291
Ida&Billy Architects
Ida Sze, Billy Chan
Project: Bridged House
Project Location: Hong Kong

292 — 297
Nota Architects
Shiyun Qian
Project: Seesaw the Garden
Project Location: Suzhou

298 — 303
MAD Architects
Ma Yansong, Dang Qun, Yosuke Hayano
Project: YueCheng Courtyard Kindergarten
Project Location: Beijing

304 — 309
Praxis d'Architecture
Shaohua Di, Xinxin Xu, Xuewei Zhang, Jialin Yang
Project: Tian Yun Industrial Office Complex
Project Location: Beijing

310 — 315
Hui Wang | Urbanus
Hui Wang
Project: Botanic Garden Expo 2019
Project Location: Beijing

316 — 321
AZL Architects
Lei Zhang
Project: CIPEA No.4 House
Project Location: Nanjing

Studio | Project

322 — 327

Studio Zhu Pei

Pei Zhu

Project: Jingdezhen Imperial Kiln Museum
Project Location: Jingdezhen

328 — 333

Turenscape

Kongjian Yu

Project: Moon-Floating Temple
Project Location: Suining

334 — 339

Wutopia Lab

Ting Yu, Erni Min

Project: Eight Tenths Garden
Project Location: Shanghai

340 — 345

Atelier Archiplein

Feng Yang, Marlène Leroux, Francis Jacquier, Fang Weiyi, Wang Mingbo

Project: Tianzhushan Tourist Infrastructure
Project Location: Tianzhushan Mountain

346 — 349

Studio Index

349 — 351

Picture Credits

The New Creative Power in Architecture

It was not until 1994 that it became possible again to run private architectural practices in China. Since then, one or two generations of young architects have turned the world's prevailing image of Chinese architecture upside down. In the mid-1990s, architecture from China was still mostly thought of as standardized, tile-clad mass housing and a few lighthouse projects, such as the Oriental Pearl Radio & TV Tower (1991–1995, picture page 20) by Huan Cheng Jiang and Shanghai Modern Architectural Design Co. Ltd. From the second half of the decade, spectacular buildings were already being built by mostly international offices from the West, such as in the financial district of Pudong in Shanghai (picture page 21 from left to right): the twin towers of the Shanghai International Finance Center by César Pelli & Associates (2004–2009), the postmodern Jin Mao Tower by SOM (Adrian D. Smith, 1994–1998), the World Financial Center by Kohn Pedderson Fox with its trapezoidal portal (1997–2008), and the twisted Shanghai Tower by Gensler (2008–2015), now China's tallest building, third tallest in the world.

At that time, China became the most dynamic country for architectural development in the world. By 2016, the German firm gmp alone had designed around 100 buildings for China and implemented numerous significant buildings with forms that simplified typical symbols or building traditions. This phase of imported architecture culminated with the CCTV Headquarters in Beijing by Rem Koolhaas' Office for Metropolitan Architecture (2002–2012). Ole Scheren, the partner at OMA responsible for

Office for Metropolitan Architecture: CCTV Headquarters, Beijing 2012

the building, has been running his own architectural practice with offices in Beijing and Hong Kong since 2010. At the beginning of the millennium, important offices founded by Chinese architects outside China also moved back to China, such as fcjz as early as 1993. Twenty years later, MAD Architects would become the first Chinese firm to beat out the top tier of Western architects in a major competition in the West at the Absolute Towers in Mississauga, Canada. In the meantime, there are numerous smaller offices that operate independently of the large official institutes in terms of design and are the foundation of the reputation that Chinese modernism enjoys today. They are dealing with their own history once again and in a completely different way, often – and in contrast to what is shown here in the book – using the less regimented architecture away from the big cities as a field for experimentation.

The History

Historical Chinese architecture clearly differs from Western architectural history, not only formally, but also in its course. For here, of course, other epoch classifications apply, but also other classification systems. While in the West it was primarily the support system that indicated or ushered in paradigm shifts over the centuries – from the various columns with entarsis, to buttresses, to round columns – in the Asian region it is the roof forms that enable distinctions to be made. Accordingly, traditional Chinese buildings emphasize the horizontal in particular, while in the West it is only at the beginning of modernity that this has surpassed the vertical or balance as a principle of form. The wall as mass plays a subordinate role in China. Symmetry, on the other hand, is initially predominant in both traditions for a long time. While in the West it was overcome by the Arts-and-Crafts, in China, on the other hand, an asymmetrical element can be found in the gardens long before and is part of the overall design. Typical materials are wood and gray or red brick, while yellow brick was reserved for the emperor. Historic houses were usually U-shaped around a courtyard, closed on the fourth side by a wall and gate. Between the Opium War and the founding of the People's Republic of China, distinctly Western buildings then sporadically appeared in the major cities, such as embassies, theaters, later cinemas, and hotels or department stores. Especially in the enclaves of the concession and crown colony areas, purely Western buildings were built, such as the Christ the King Church in Tsingtau by the German Curt Rothkegel, who worked in China from 1903 to 1929 and was even asked to build a parliament building in 1910.

The Early 20th Century

In the early 20th century, Western influence became more apparent as a first generation of Chinese architects graduated in the United States or Europe. Mediated by America, schools of architecture emerged in succession to the French Beaux-Arts academies, and a Western style of architecture emerged that often appeared Chinese only in the roof – the traditional distinguishing feature – or in decorative applications. But classical modernism also moved in: In Shanghai Jiangwan, an Art Deco district was built in the 1930s under President Chiang Kai-Shek. The architect Dayou Dong, who had studied in Minneapolis, built the old city hall in a mix of international modernist and Art Deco with classical Chinese architecture. A critical modernism was discussed. A next generation of architects came to America in the second half of the 1940s and met the modernist elite who had fled Europe, especially Germany, to escape the Nazis, such as Walter Gropius, Marcel Breuer and Mies van der Rohe. Among the Chinese students Gropius taught at the Harvard Graduate School of Design between 1937 and 1952 was Ieoh Ming Pei *, the most famous Chinese architect in the second half of the 20th century.

Postwar Modernism of the People's Republic

With the founding of the People's Republic of China in 1949, the framework conditions for architects in China had changed fundamentally. In 1952, private architectural firms were banned and large municipal, university or state design institutes took over their functions: Architects became engineers (gongchengshi). The planning economy significantly changed the development of architecture and took up similar formal principles that can also be found in the West: for example, the disappearance of the roof or functional urban planning in the wake of the ideas of the Athens Charter, mediated by the Soviet Union. During the Great Proletarian Cultural Revolution (1966–1976), even architects who had previously built representative buildings of the young state ran into problems, such as Bó Zhāng, who had built the neoclassical Hall of the National People's Congress in Beijing in 1958. However, the rigid and megalomaniacal neo-classicism common to many young states remained and continues to be evident two decades later at the Mausoleum of Mao Zedong.

Ieoh Ming Pei

Even before the official end of the Cultural Revolution, I. M. Pei returned to China for the first time in 1974, after Richard Nixon's visit to China in 1972 had significantly improved relations between the states. For decades, he was the epitome of Chinese architecture beyond the construction offices for the West. Pei grew up in a historic house in the 14th-century Lion Groove

Bó Zhāng: Hall of the National People's Congress, Beijing 1958

Garden in Suzhou, which his grandfather bought in 1917 – now a Unesco World Heritage Site and one of the most outstanding gardens of the period. Impressed by Shanghai's first skyscrapers, he began studying architecture in the 1930s at the rather conservative MIT in Philadelphia. After World War II, he continued master's studies as a fellow at Harvard under Gropius, and after graduation also worked as an outside consultant for The Architects Collaborative (TAC). Gropius was particularly interested in prefabricated housing units in the 1940s, which worked well with Chinese spatial dispositions as well as their traditional wood construction methods. However, Pei was of the opinion that the International Style could not be transferred so easily to all parts of the world and was therefore rather impressed by the compositions of Ludwig Mies van der Rohe. Mies, who had been teaching in Chicago since 1939, placed far more emphasis on merging the modular with the aesthetic. His great interest in the relationship of the building to the open space also suited all Chinese architects, since the connection between nature and culture is a characteristic of the Chinese tradition. Pei's work is characterized by a great interest in large geometric forms and with this he was the personification of modern Chinese architecture in the West for decades. In 1985–1990, Pei built the Bank of China Tower in Hong Kong when talks were already underway to return the city to the People's Republic.

Ieoh Ming Pei: Main entrance of the Louvre-restructuring, Paris 1989

The Turnaround

In 1978, Deng Xiaoping* had proclaimed Socialism with Chinese Characteristics at the 3rd Plenary Session of the XI Central Committee. This reform and opening-up developed into economic pragmatism with personal freedoms under the leadership of the Chinese Communist Party. In 1994, a regulation for the licensing of architects followed, who initially could only appear as façade designers for design institutes in larger construction projects. For private clients (Xishu Bookstore by fcjz) and away from high-speed urbanism, however, opportunities arose for experimental architecture. In 1999, a UIA congress was held in Beijing and for the first time a larger group of international architects visited the city, followed by the 2004 Architecture Biennale held simultaneously here and in Venice. As early as 2002, the monthly magazine World Architecture (editor: Lu Wang) offered the first WA Chinese Architecture Award, chaired by Wilfried Wang. Away from the international commissions for the lighthouse projects, a domestic scene is emerging that was initially also received abroad, but has now blossomed over the past ten years to such an extent that it is also clearly perceived in China. And in implementations and designs – also and especially in complex fields such as parametric architecture – they have been able to keep up with the avant-garde right from the start. As recently as 2008, Herzog & de Meuron called on Ai Weiwei* as an experienced artistic advisor for the stadium of the 2008 Olympic Games. Today, a local architect would probably build it ...

The Pragmatism

China's international success in architecture has various reasons, but they can be subsumed under the term pragmatism. On the one hand, there are the young architects who have often learned abroad. On the other hand, there are architects from abroad who are fully committed to the local conditions. You may not be able to create an entire project, but decisive parts, even if in the end a construction manager decides on unconfirmed changes ad hoc. That the half-life is much shorter than some Western architects would like: 30 years, in the case of interiors much less, must suffice. That the protection of historical monuments and the participation of the population are significantly lower and that environmental awareness has an even less comprehensive status. But all this means that young offices can and

Skyline of Shanghai from the Bund

are allowed to build things more quickly. And among them – as this volume shows – there is an architecture that increasingly mediates between modernity and Chinese architectural tradition, that turns to regional typologies, rediscovers traditional craft techniques and handles old substance with great care, as Taining Cheng and Wang Shu* demanded.

Coordination Asia

Zhang Lin

Tilman Thürmer

a **Shanghai Museum of Glass**
Location
Shanghai
Completion 2011, 2017

b **Art Plaza**
Location
Shanghai
Completion 2019

c **Design Wing**
Location
Shanghai
Completion 2016

Coordination Asia was founded in 2009 by Tilman Thürmer, born in 1972. He is Vice President of the Shanghai Museum of Glass and has worked together with its president Zhang Lin, born in 1965, for more than a decade on its creation. The studio is an award-winning international agency, specialized in creating curated experiences and bold environments for museums, exhibitions and brands. The studio's Shanghai-based practice is known for its content-driven approach and innovative design solutions. Its passion lies in creating meaningful connections between people, places and their stories. As an all-around design consultancy, Coordination Asia provides a range of services from the initiation of a project to the completion, also including brand consulting, curation, design conceptualization and detail design, realization, and supervision.

a

b

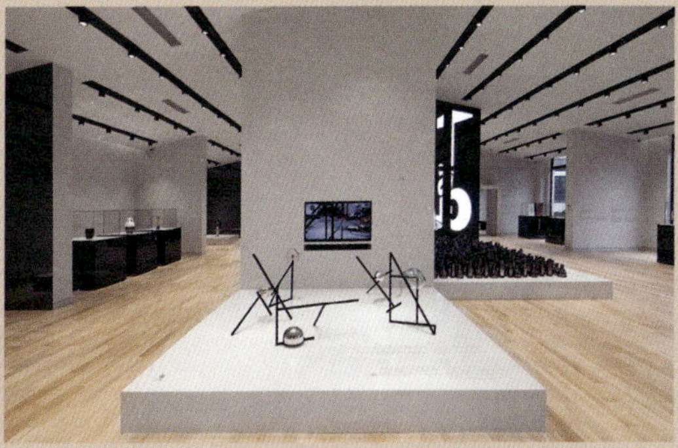
c

Rainbow Chapel

Location
685 Changjiang West Road, Baoshan District, Shanghai 200431, China
Building type religious
Completion 2015
Client Shanghai G+ Culture Creative Developing Co., Ltd
Gross floor area 390 m^2

a

b

The Rainbow Chapel is placed inside the Shanghai Museum of Glass Park and unveils an unique lifestyle destination in China. The building is enclosed by laminated glass panels in vivid, yet translucent colors, which create a surreal light. The façade pattern is made of 3,060 elements using 65 different colors, and the semi-transparent kaleidoscope windows of 6.8 meters in height give the Rainbow Chapel an uplifting vibe. With the movement of the sun the lighting in the chapel changes as well. The chapel is set inside a square in the form of a semi-open frame and picks up the forms of square and circle as two fundamental shapes to Chinese symbolism. While the circle stands for fullness and unity, the square is a symbol for honesty and virtue. The two shapes combined provide the place with a spirit of luck. The construction is surrounded by a water passage. As an addition a multifunctional hall for events and banquets is set next to the building. The project is meant to establish the Shanghai Museum of Glass Park as a significant cultural and lifestyle destination in the city.

a Front view on the chapel
b Colorful interior design
c Semi-transparent windows
d View inside
e Floor plan
f Light falling through window

c

d

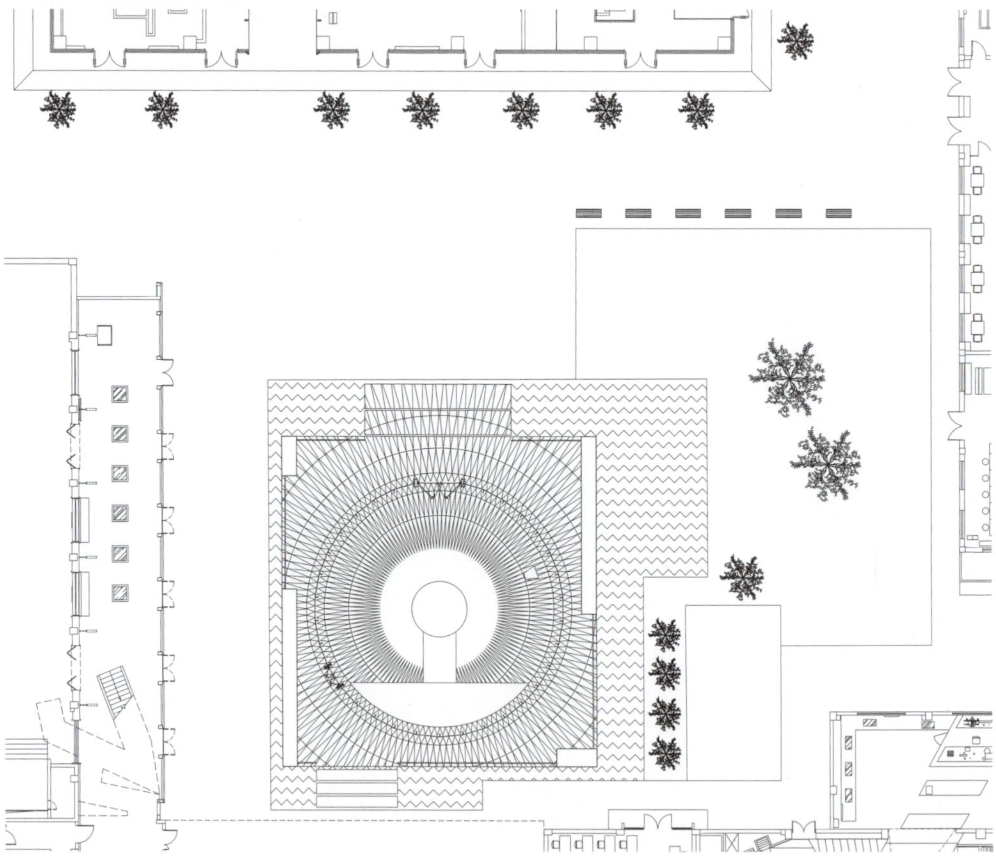

e

Bao Wei Architecture Office

Wei Bao

a **No.66 Lanman Hutong**
Location
Beijing
Completion 2017

b **Noah Farming Visitor Center**
Location
Beijing
Completion 2016

c **Hutong Exhibition Pavilion**
Location
Beijing
Completion 2019

d **Muai Thai Space**
Location
Beijing
Completion 2017

BWAO (Bao Wei Architecture Office) was established in Beijing in 2013. As founding member and principal, Bao Wei, born in 1982, got his MArch degree with distinction from Harvard Graduate School of Design and BArch degree from School of Architecture, Tsinghua University. BWAO's practice involves mainly with projects that intertwine with rich urban and cultural context. The studio approaches design from a very fundamental level, be it programmatic challenges, site responses, or client aspirations. In the eyes of the office the way a project is executed is born out of a design synthesis that searches for the fittest solution, more like a scientific experiment. As a result, each project is recognized with its unique intellectual intensity and formal identity. BWAO believes that the design exists transcendentally on site and sees it as an architect's role to excavate and present it carefully.

a

b

c

d

Bao Wei
Architecture Office

Location
Changping District, Beijing, China
Building type office
Completion 2019
Client confidential
Gross floor area 180 m²

Rooftop House

a

b

The client is a tech company that occupies an entire office building. A rooftop house was built to provide a home-like space for its staff members. The building mass is maximized within a setback limit and shaped by views out to the city or the mountains in the background. Three courtyards with different identities were introduced to create internalized landscapes. All programs are choreographed in ways to take full advantage of either corner views out or courtyard views within. The entire building is elevated on a datum in order to gain a vantage point, bypassing the parapets of the existing building that block the views. The cavity space in-between the new floor plate and existing roof not only helps with the thermal performance of the new house, but also provides depth for earth and water features of the courtyards and space for air-conditioning ducts that feed into the rooms.

a View back to the kitchen
b Water courtyard
c Entry view into the kitchen
d Living area
e Lounge area
f Building floor plan
g Exploded axiometry view

c

d

e

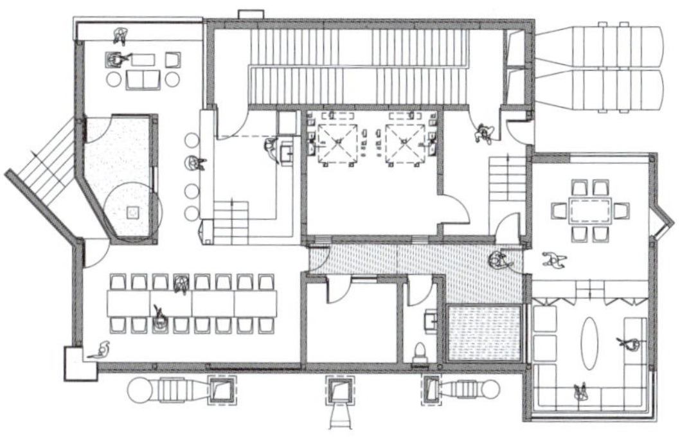

f

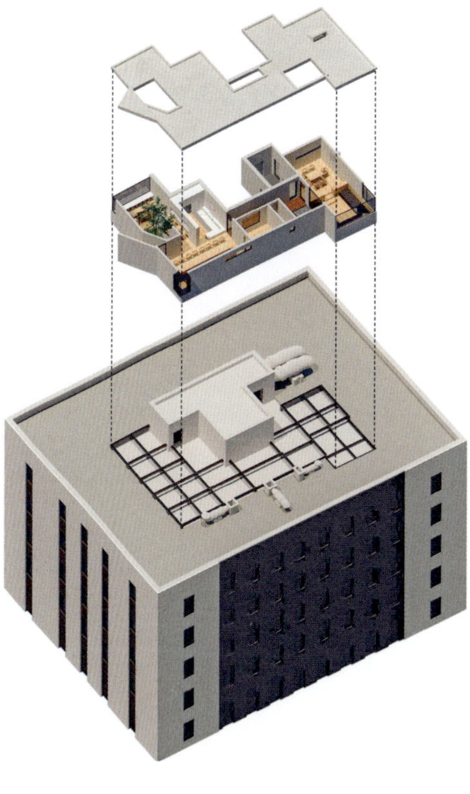

g

LLab.

David Correa, Taichi Kuma

Hanxiao Liu, Luís Ricardo

a **Beigala, The Nostalgic Station**
Location
Beigou Village
Completion 2018

b **Bamboo Bamboo Canopy and Pavilions**
Location
Yangshuo, Guilin
Completion 2020

c **LEO Digital Networks Headquarter**
Location
Shanghai
Completion 2015

LLLab. is a design studio founded in 2016 and based in Shanghai, Stuttgart and Porto operating within the fields of architecture, design, art, urbanism, research and development. The studio is led by four partners: Hanxiao Liu, born in 1985, Luís Ricardo, born in 1985, David Correa born in 1981 and Taichi Kuma, born in 1985. The studio's projects have been widely published in international press including Archdaily, Domus and Frame, while their design research work has been featured at multiple international venues including the Keller Gallery at MIT Massachusetts Institute of Technology and the Bozar Center for Fine Arts in Brussels. Their work focuses on using design as a tool to improve social and cultural life through various scales. The principals are driven by an experimental and playful approach that leads to well-executed design projects.

a

b

c

San Sa Village

Location
Beigou Village, Huairou District, Beijing, China
Building type recreational
Completion 2019
Client 2049 Investment Group
Gross floor area 1,600 m²

a

b

San Sa Village was built as a rural oasis with the aim to provide visitors with a spatial and sensory experience. To embed an appreciation for the site's heritage, the existing spatial arrangement of the village was extended, scattering the architectural blocks in-line with the typical village plan, while combining those blocks into an integrated whole. By subverting the stereotypical concept of rural tourism resorts, the idea was to create a kind of village within a village and to give the piece of land the vitality it deserves. The design complies with the basic elements and volume division of the original village and aims to simplify architectural details in order to facilitate the use of local resources. Many local, authentic and readily available materials were used during the production. The landscape design was directed by San She Inn Cultural Management. For construction the team was fully integrated with modern management and local villagers' practices. The layout of the design aims to make the ecology of buildings and courtyards different from other typical buildings in North China. The goal was to embrace the five senses of the visitor by creating a surrounding for self-reflection and conscious engagement with the environment. Spaces like the courtyards in between the buildings are supposed to make one feel no longer disturbed by neighbors but furthermore give visitors an option to sit in a quiet place where they can forget about time.

a Top view east courtyard
b View over the village in the village
c Top view courtyard
d Detail drawing
e Private corners of the houses
f Deep courtyard in the west
g General plan
h Terrace on the tea house

c

d

e

f

g h

DnA_Design and Architecture

Xu Tiantian

a **Tofu Factory**
Location
Caizhai Village
Completion 2018

b **Wangjing Memorial**
Location
Wang Village
Completion 2017

c **Shimen Bridge**
Location
Shimen and Shimenyu Village
Completion 2017

d **Bamboo Theater**
Location
Hengkeng Village
Completion 2016

DnA_Design and Architecture, situated in Chaoyang District, is an interdisciplinary practice addressing the contemporary living environment, both physical and social, from small to large scales. It was established in 2004 by Xu Tiantian, born in 1975. For the studio the approach to projects starts with research and discussion on context, program and their interaction which they believe to be the fundamental elements or the DNA that will define design and architecture to adapt, engage, and contribute to our society of multiplicity and complexity. Context, program, and their potential relationship will cultivate architecture into a multidimensional expression and generate a new experiment and exploration for users. Architecture is seen as an influence and inspiration to the contemporary life.

a

b

c

d

Dushan Leisure Center

Location
Dushan Mountain, Songyang County, Lishui, Zhejiang, China
Building type culture
Completion 2018
Client Tourism Development Cooperation Limited of Songyang County
Gross floor area 1,647 m²

a

b

Dushan Leisure Center located at the foot of Dushan Mountain adjacent to the Songyin River is one of the key tourism projects of the Songyin River Scenic District Development. It contains a visitor center, water sports facilities and a gym for water sports athletes. The entire triangular harbor is being considered as a waterpark for tourists and local communities alike and therefore a meeting point for both groups. The architectural programs are organized through a spiral with the visitor facilities at the center and the gym at the far end, connected by an east-west walkway as a shortcut. A C-shaped dike connects to the Songyin River and will also become the passage for pedestrians, bicycles and tourism electric shuttles. The overall configuration provides an undulating walkway for above the harbor, with constantly changing views of the mountain and water. The project adopts timber structure as natural material, low-carbon construction, and traditional special quality. Glass curtain walls with a different gradient of translucency bring subtle shift on building façades as misty surfaces on the water. Layers of indoor and outdoor space create an interplay of views like the traditional Chinese landscape garden. The meditation room on the second floor is also a multifunction room. The opening on the roof casts the trace of sun on the floor with bronze plates of different hours in the Chinese 24 solar terms, creating a dialogue with the nature and time.

a Outer façade
b Meditation room
c South entrance view
d Exploded axonometric view
e Interior design
f Interior view from another room
g Exterior front view

c

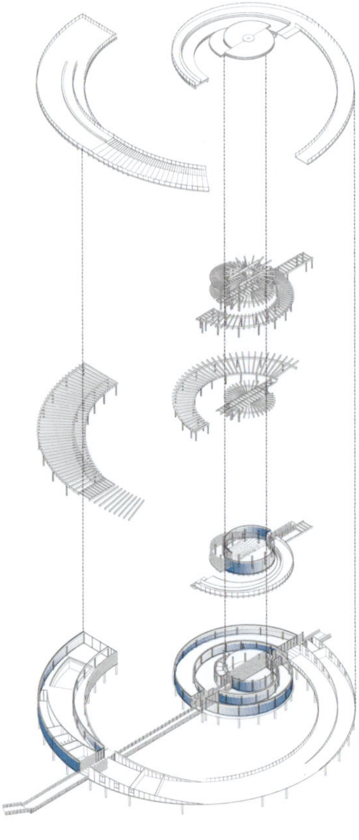

d

e f

g

People's Architecture Office

James Shen

Zhe He

Feng Zang

a **People's Station**
Location
Yantai
Completion 2017

b **Courtyard House Plugin Office**
Location
Beijing
Completion 2013

c **Lakeside Plugin Tower**
Location
Beijing
Completion 2017

People's Architecture Office, short PAO, is an international practice with offices based in Beijing, China and Boston, USA. Founded in 2010 by Zhe He, born in 1978, James Shen, born in 1977, and Feng Zang, born in 1978, the firm is a multidisciplinary studio focused on social impact through design particularly in the areas of housing, urban regeneration, and education. People's Architecture Office is the first architecture firm certified as a B-Corporation in Asia and serves as a model social enterprise. Domus named PAO as one of the world's best architecture firms of 2019 and Fast Company listed the studio as one of the world's ten most innovative architecture companies in 2018. The studio's award-winning works have been exhibited at the Venice Architecture Biennale, Harvard Graduate School of Design and the London Design Museum.

a

b

c

Location
Shenzhen, China
Building type residential
Completion 2018
Client Guanhu Subdistrict /
FuturePlus Academy
Gross floor area 44.6 m²

Shangwei Village Plugin Houses

a

b

The Shangwei Village Plugin Houses revitalizes old houses that left were vacant and in ruins after Shangwei Village suffered from heavy disinvestment. The project consists of two different houses: one belonging to Mr. Fang with a gross floor area of 25.8 square meters and the other one belonging to Mr. Huang with a gross floor area of 18.8 square meters. The Fang family house can be seen here on the pages 48 and 49, while the pages 50 and 51 show the house of the Huang family. The rapid urban expansion of nearby Shenzhen engulfed villages like Shangwei, turning them into urban villages or rural islands surrounded by a sea of new development. The project was therefore created in response to the homes in Shangwei Village being vacant and difficult to renovate because any work would affect adjacent structures. To circumvent this problem, the Plugin Houses leave the original structure untouched while a new structure is built inside an existing house. The planning for this was realized by FuturePlus Academy. A modular building system of prefabricated panels was used, making it possible to affordably and efficiently upgrade dilapidated buildings to modern living.

a Bird's-eye view Fang family house
b Exterior Fang family house
c Exterior Huang family house
d Bird's-eye view Huang family house
e Interior Huang family house
f Interior Huang family house
g Detail

c

d

e

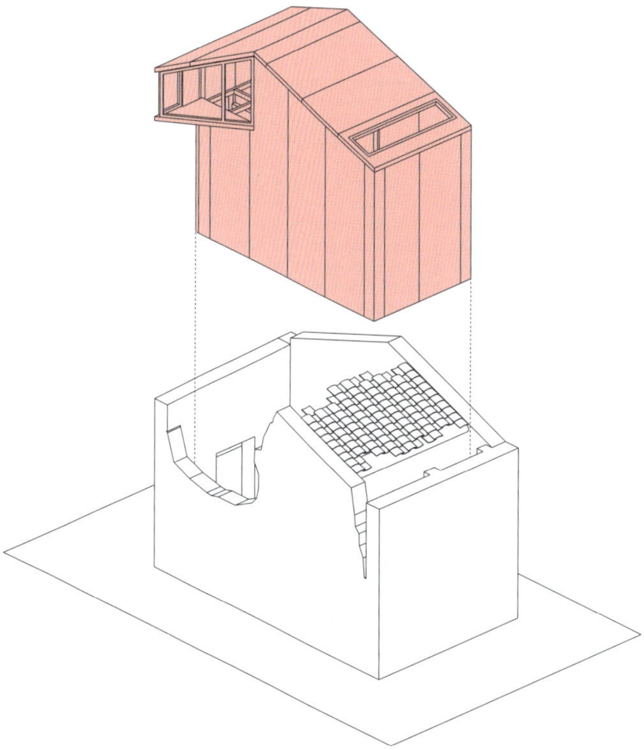

f g

3andwich Design

Wei He

Long Chen

a **B Garden**
Location
Xinyang
Completion 2017

b **Stone Nest Amphitheater**
Location
Wujiatuan Village
Completion 2019

c **Shangping Village Regeneration**
Location
Xijuan
Completion 2017

d **Restoration and Reconstruction of Geng Tang Hall**
Location
Hongguan Village
Completion 2019

3andwich Design was founded in 2012 by Wei He, born in 1973, and Long Chen, born in 1990. The studio gets supported from authoritative academic institutions including Central Academy of Fine Arts, Tsinghua University, and China Architectural Society. Their design concept emphasizes humanism, dialogue between history and contemporary, and interaction between natural environment and regional culture. 3andwich Design focuses on cross-border thinking and dedication to rural architecture design especially in undeveloped areas of China. The studio not only pays attention to the preliminary planning and construction on site but also to the linkage between management and media communication. It regards these sections as an interrelated whole as it believes that architectural design should embrace relevant disciplines and integrate them.

a

b

c

d

Limestone Gallery

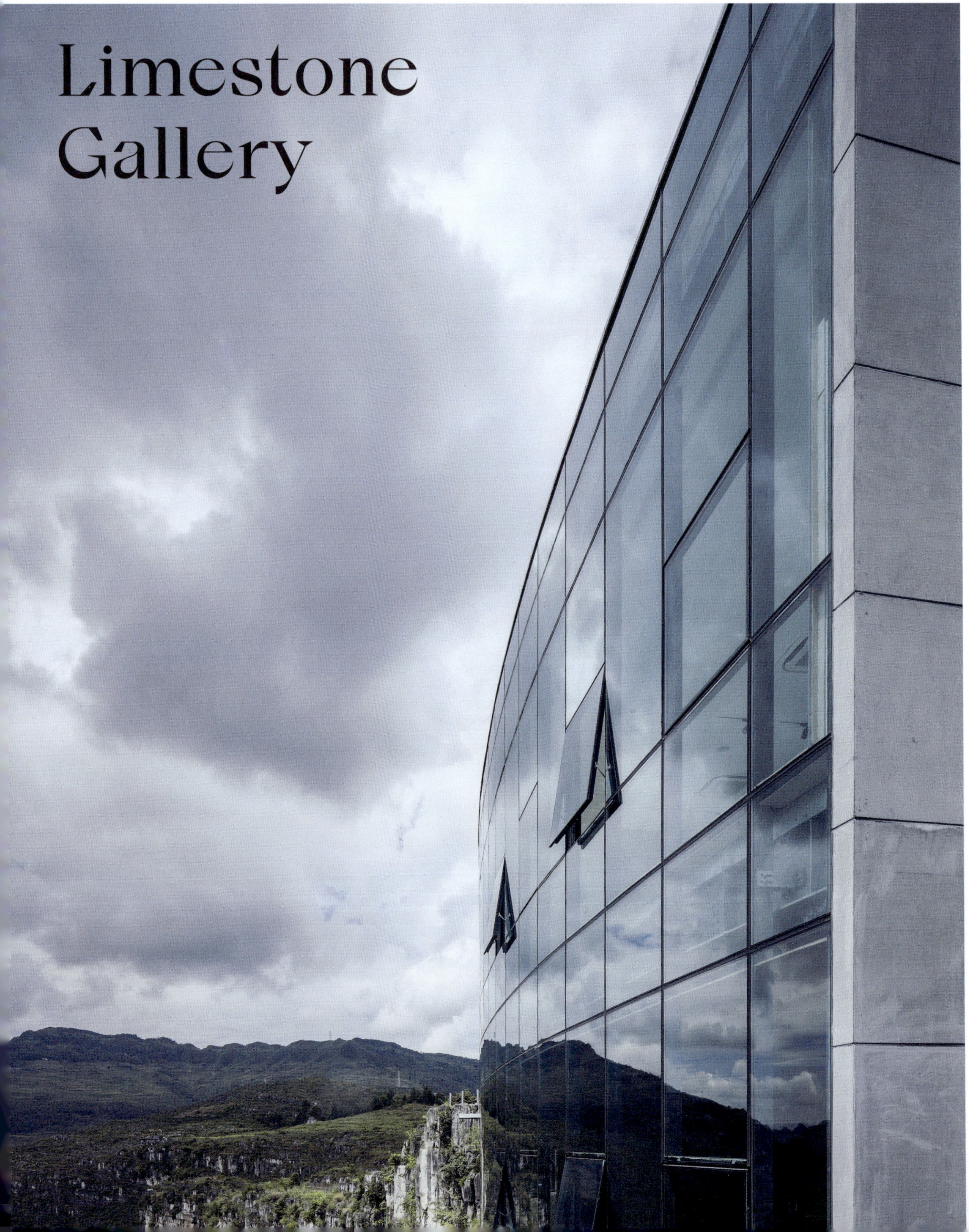

Location
Dushan Town, Anlong County, China
Building type culture
Completion 2017
Client Anlong Heyun Tourism and Cultural Development Co., Ltd
Gross floor area 1,350 m^2

a

b

Limestone Gallery is located on the Haiwei Canyon which has become a paradise for outdoor sports like rock climbing. It is surrounded by mountains and lies above a river meandering from hundreds of miles away. The building was constructed together with the Mountain Journey company and the TYMJ Home Furnishing studio in the shape of a non-symmetrical crescent and contains two floors, including different areas for exhibition, conference and service. The very bottom floor is designed as an outdoor lounge space. A large part of the construction work, such as site leveling and large size materials transporting, was done manually by local labors, due to the particular location of the site. The façade of Limestone Gallery was designed with curved glass walls, offering a contrast to the solid mountains around. Through the reflection of the glass the building seems to be hidden on top of the cliff. Visitors can experience a magnificent panoramic view of the Haiwei Canyon from the rooftop which is being used as a viewing point. From there one can see the Tourists' Center which was also created by 3andwich Design studio.

a Limestone Gallery from above
b Lounge area
c Side view on the gallery
d Lounge area with furniture
e Sightseeing platform
f Gallery cross section
g First floor plan

c

d

e 

f

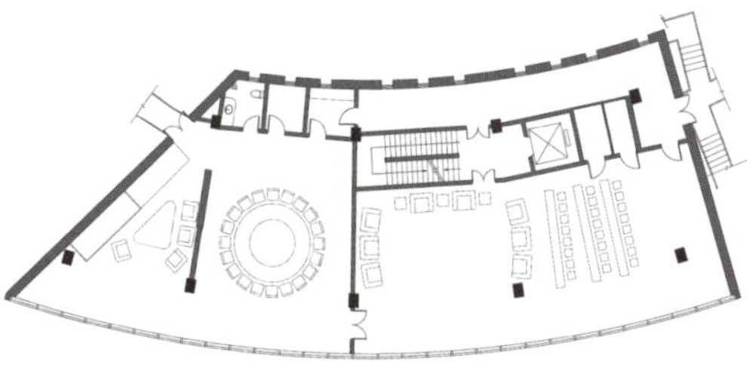

g

RooMoo Design

Tao Zhang, Marine Bois

Hui Zhang, Rui Zhang

a **Whatever Eyewear**
Location
Shanghai
Completion 2019

b **LeCoq in Urbn Hotel**
Location
Shanghai
Completion 2020

c **LeCoq Wine&Bistro**
Location
Shanghai
Completion 2018

RooMoo Design Studio was founded in Shanghai in 2015 by Hui Zhang, born 1987, Rui Zhang, born 1984, Tao Zhang, born 1984, and Marine Bois, born 1987. The office is based on a definite relationship between architecture, interior and product design, which has been a driving force to create projects with subtle transitions between these disciplines. The studio pursues the integrity and the quality of the design from the beginning of a project until accomplishment. The understanding of the local culture and of internationalization, makes RooMoo Design Studio explore the critical point in between. They challenge traditional boundaries to new contemporary perspectives re-using a local culture touch in modern design. Since 2015, the studio's projects have been recognized by many professional design media.

a

b

c

RooMoo Design

Canada Goose Shanghai Office

Location
Jingan District, Shanghai, China
Building type office
Completion 2019
Client Canada Goose
Gross floor area 480 m²

The Canada Goose Shanghai Office – a luxury outdoor brand – was established in two blocks of recently renovated historical old warehouses of the 1920s–1930s in a new office park. The two buildings have different levels. The main entrance is located in Block C, at the second level of this block a staircase links to the second level of Block A where the main open workspaces are located. Here, an external terrace and an outdoor staircase next to the open workspaces create a secondary entrance to the office. The building was originally used as practice rooms for the former Shanghai People's Acrobatic Troupe. The intention of this renovation work is to respect the old architectural spirit and at the same time give it a new life and warm feeling with a modern touch. The façade textures are kept as the original, the renovation work plays a subtle role. Brick and steel are the main materials. At the main entrance a new made brick wall with full height is playing a contrast to the historical elements. Coming into the heart of this block, a shared core is visually connecting the pantry to the very top of this building, almost like a chimney place in a condo: This emphasizes the place where meetings and gathers happen. The brown metal elements are used both indoor and outdoor. They connect all parts of the building and tell the old construction from the new.

a Ground floor plan
b First floor plan
c Main entrance
d Connections between two levels
e Second floor plan
f Third floor plan
g Pantry area
h Meeting room and pantry area
i Open workspace

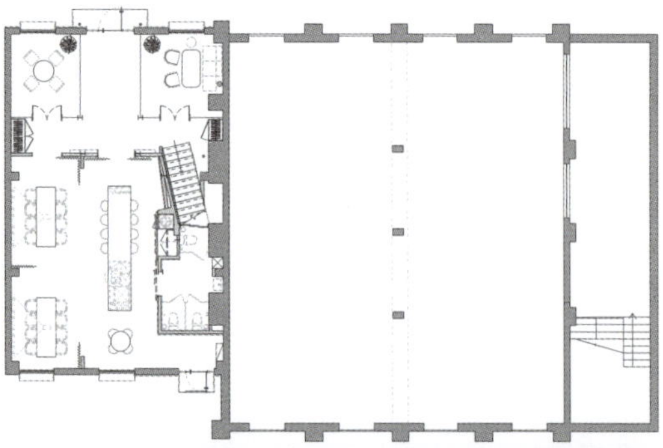

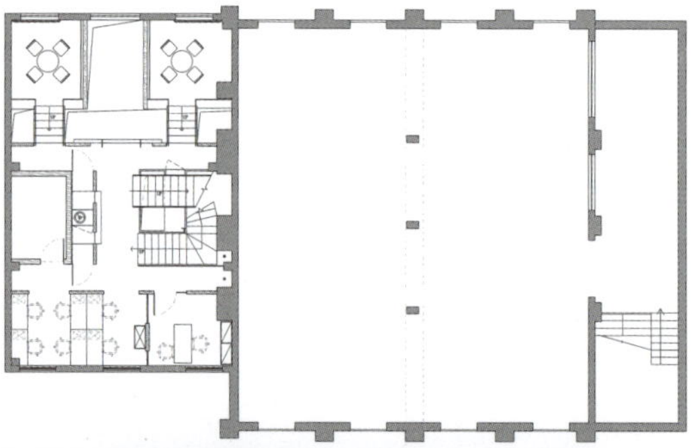

a b

c d

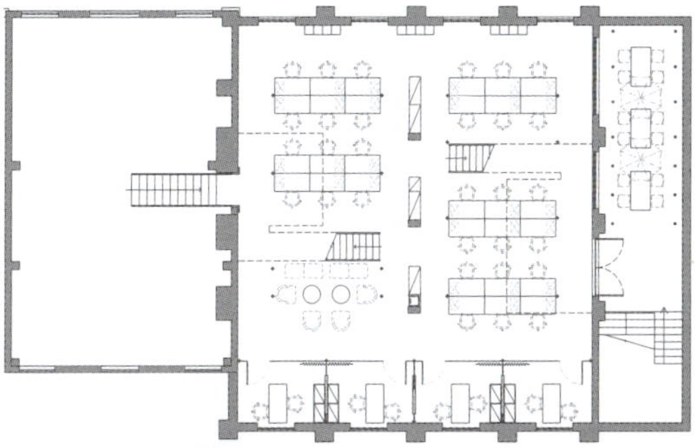

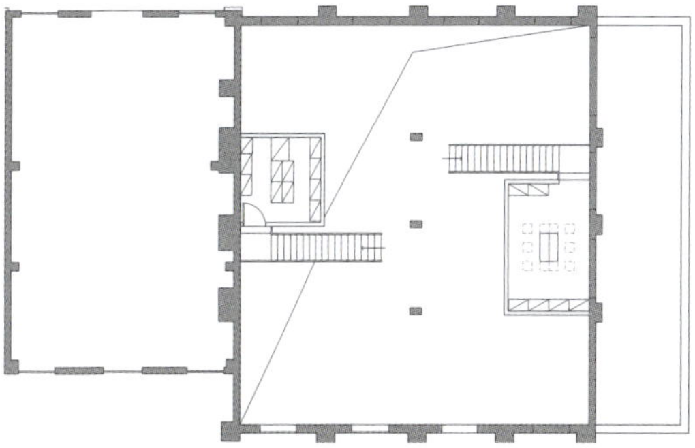

e f

g h

i

Taolei Architectural Design

Tao Lei

a **The Concave House**
Location
Benxi
Completion 2010

b **CAFA Shandong Art Education Center**
Location
Jinan
Completion 2020

c **Yue Art Gallery**
Location
Beijing
Completion 2011

Tao Lei, born in 1976, founded Taolei Architectural Design, short TAOA, in 2011. The studio seeks a new way of architecture which not only coexists with the natural environment but can adapt itself to the future. Based on the combination of traditional Chinese culture and modern notion, all projects designed by TAOA – including for example dwelling design and commercial center design – create free and authentic space atmosphere in an organic and relaxing way. Such a value enables TAOA to perfect every single segment of architectural practice involving project planning, conceptual design and construction detail. Furthermore the studio pays attention to the social context of architecture as well as meeting the client's demand. Tao Lei Architecture Designing Corporation has gained widely reputation in the architectural field and its works have been recognized and published widely.

a

b

c

Location
Shunyi District,
Beijing, China
Building type residential
Completion 2017
Client Tao Lei
Gross floor area 600 m^2

Own House of Architect

a

b

The building was created as an intervention in an existing detached house, leading to something completely new. The material application of wood and metal contributes to creating a truthful relationship between the building and nature. The aim of the design of this project was to unite architectural functionality and spirituality and achieve a high grade of comfort. Covering the site and the original building, a huge overlay blurs the boundary between the building and courtyard, interior and exterior, trees and natural light. This cover is trying to mix all parts into one while maintaining the self-contained characteristics of each piece of the construction. New realms are deriving and the building is no longer separating people from nature, but rejoins the two parts. In this independent world, space is free to stretch as an abstracted landscape. Artistic conceptions of Chinese landscape are interpreted by geometric space, free to wander, even being converted among different situations.

a The courtyard in autumn
b Partial view of the courtyard
c Painting room
d Outer and inner design plan
e Conversion of the original house
f Courtyard from different angle
g The sunken courtyard

c

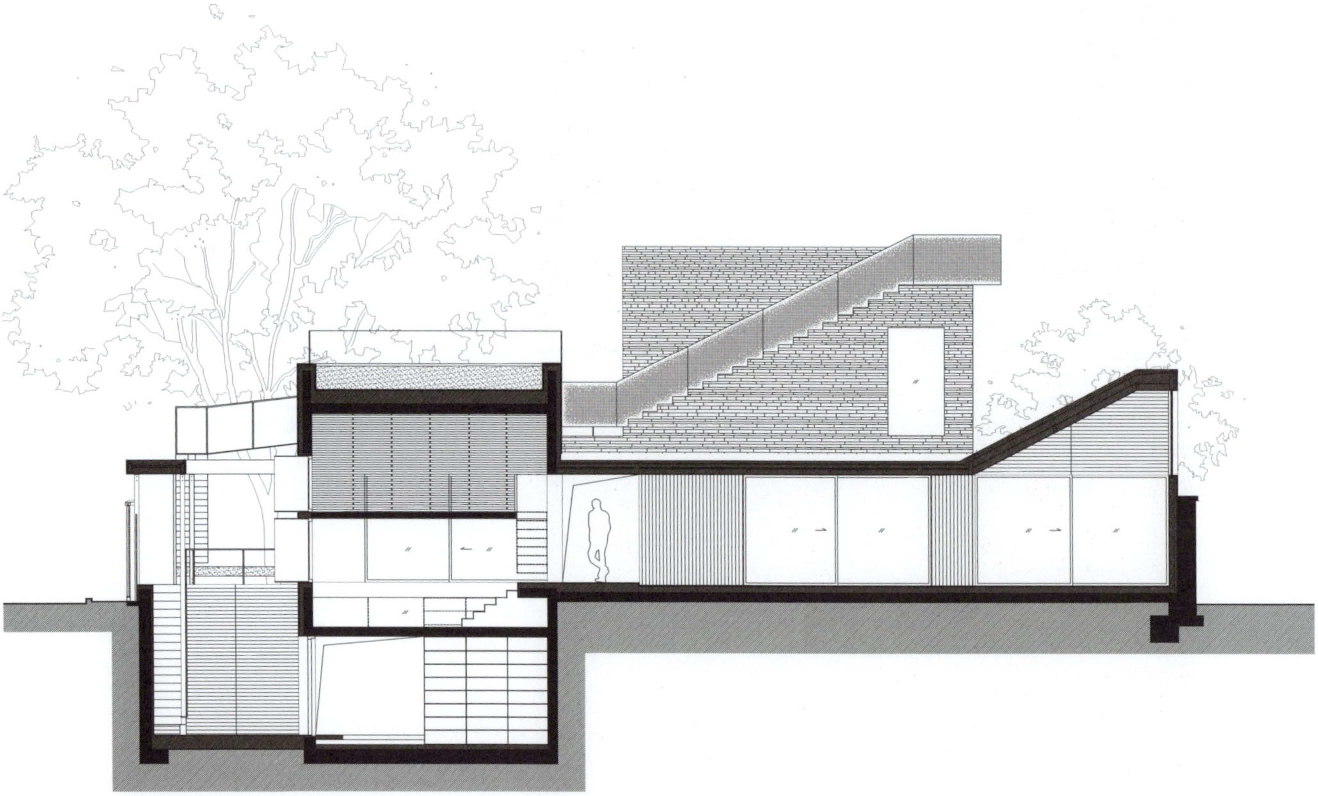

d

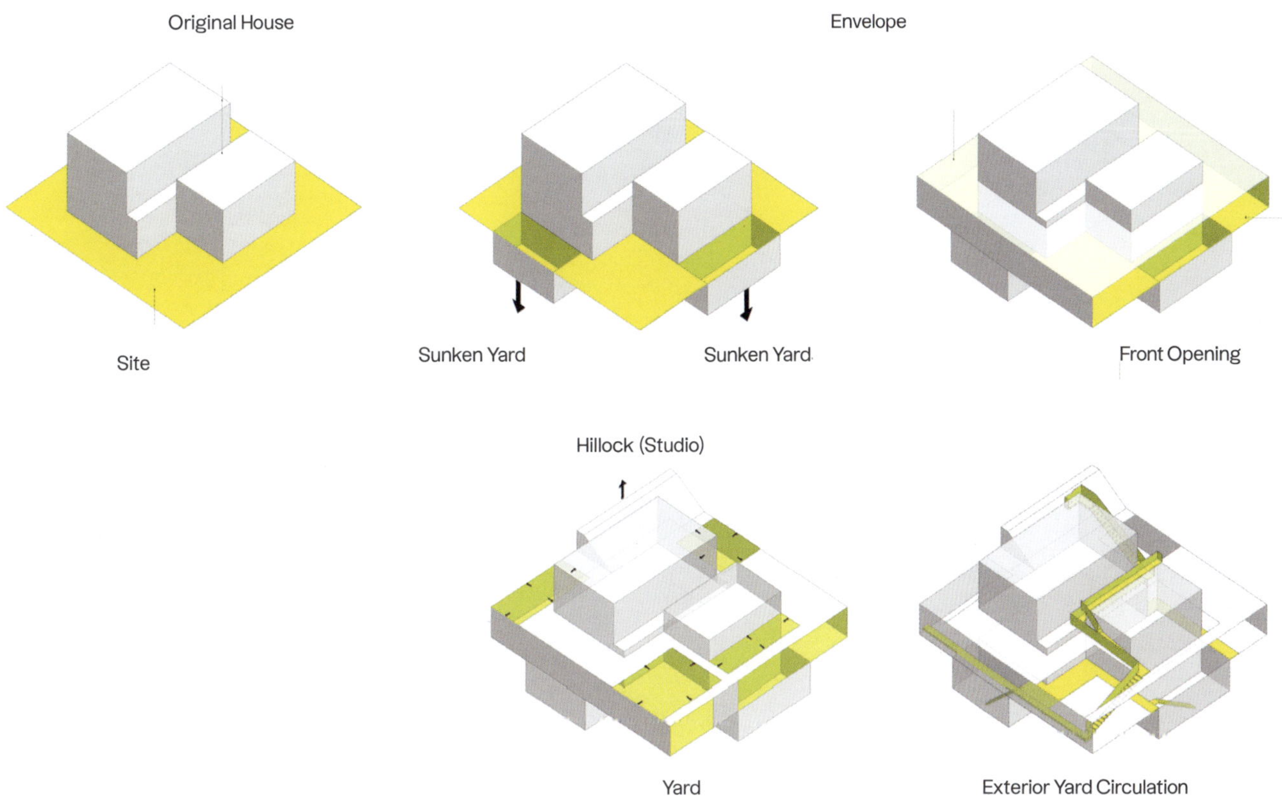
Original House
Envelope
Site
Sunken Yard
Sunken Yard
Front Opening
Hillock (Studio)
Yard
Exterior Yard Circulation

e

f g

B.L.U.E. Architecture Studio

Shuhei Aoyama

a **White Pagoda Temple Hutong Courtyard Renovation**
Location
Beijing
Completion 2018

b **M Woods Art Community**
Location
Beijing
Completion 2019

c **% Arabica**
Location
Shanghai
Completion 2019

d **Forest Valley Hot Spring Center**
Location
Chengde
Completion 2019

Founded in 2014, B.L.U.E. Architecture Studio was established in Beijing by Japanese architects Shuhei Aoyama and Yoko Fujii, both born in 1980. It is an international architecture studio full of youthfulness and vitality oriented towards architecture and architectural interior design. B.L.U.E. is the abbreviation of Beijing Laboratory for Urban Environment – the core design philosophy of the studio. Focusing on the intense collision of rich history and vanward thought of Beijing, B.L.U.E. is working on architecture, interior design, product design, and art. Researching urban physics, society, culture and environment, it connects the urban environments. With numerous international awards, B.L.U.E. participated in many exhibitions – including the Venice Biennale, 2016 – and works on projects at home and abroad.

a

b

c

d

Ota Fine Arts Gallery

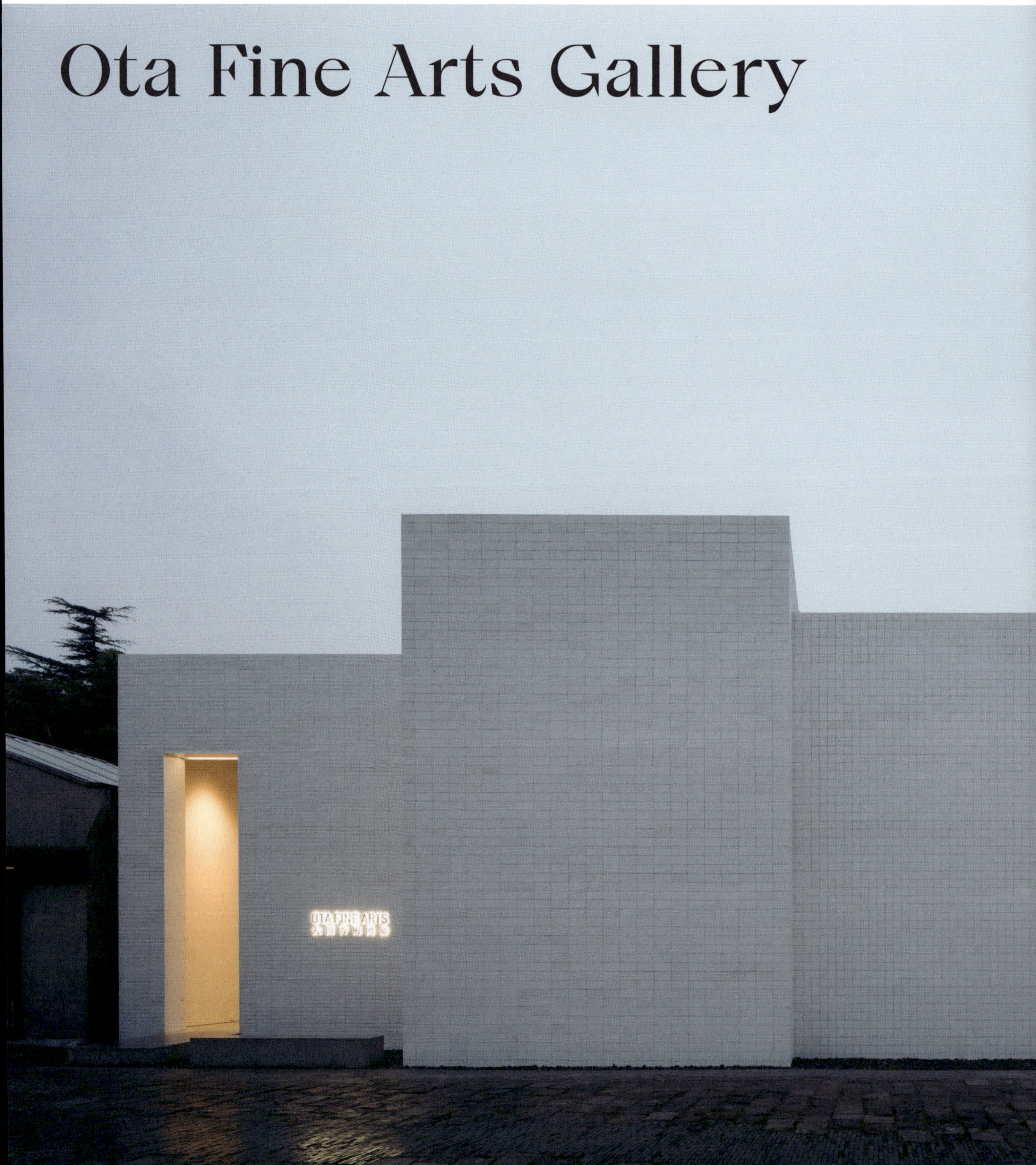

Location
West Bund, Building 3,
2555 Longteng Avenue,
Shanghai 200232, China
Building type culture
Completion 2017
Client Ota Fine Arts
Gross floor area 286.53 m^2

23 years after the founding of Ota Fine Arts, the Shanghai gallery is the first in China, following the galleries of Tokyo and Singapore. The founder, Hidenori Ota, is the most important promoter of Japan's contemporary national treasure artist Kusama Yayoi, provides a platform to more Asian cutting-edge artists and expands the new direction of the Asian contemporary art. The Shanghai gallery was a three-bay old bungalow the architects dismantled, building a brand-new and pure building. The design process began with six main functional areas required by the gallery, but was reduced to four pure big blocks. The texture of pure white bricks refers to the traditional gray brick of Shanghai traditional Shikumen-style as well as to the red brick of French villas in the colonial period. The white surface makes the building more abstract and syncretizes with the many white buildings in the modern art area of the West Bund. The eastern side of the building faces the office entrance of the West Bund staff and provides the main façade of the gallery, while the main entrance is the only opening in the western façade. Windows of different sizes create a dialogue between the interior of the building and the outdoor space.

a Eastern façade
b Exhibition hall
c Hallway
d Skylight
e White bricks
f Diagram volumes
g First floor plan
h Diagram volumes close up

a

b

c d

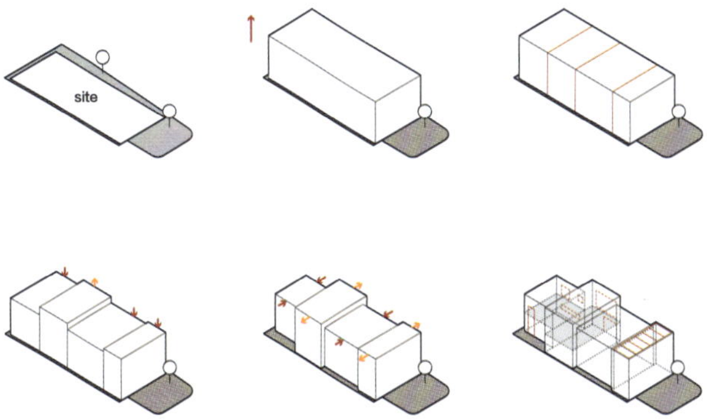

e f

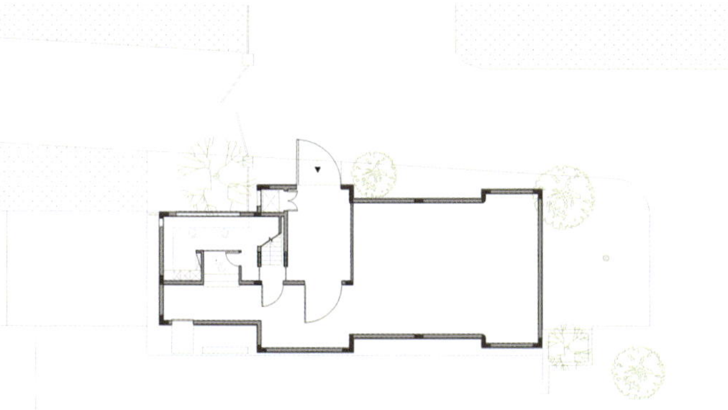

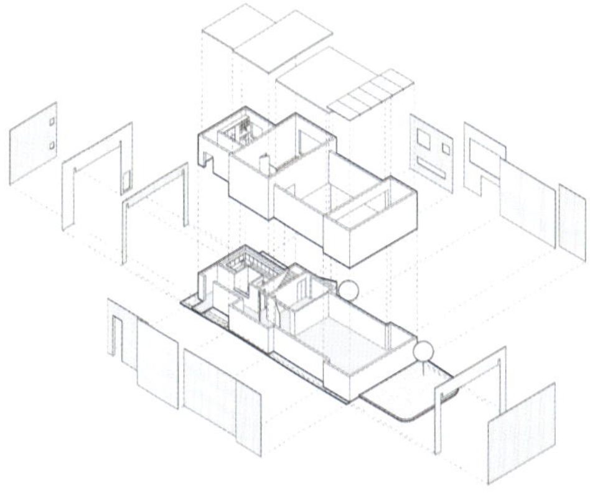

g h

Shing & Partners Design Group

Eric Shing

The studio

a The Livable Land
Location
Guangzhou
Completion 2018

b Zonco Center
Location
Hefei
Completion 2017

c Meizhou Chaotang Hotel
Location
Meizhou
Completion 2019

d Yangshuo Resort Hotel
Location
Yangshuo
Completion 2013

Shing & Partners is an award-winning design firm providing integrated professional services for urban planning, architectural design, interior design and landscape architecture. Nowadays, the company has matured to a team of 300 employees in Guangzhou and Beijing offices, consisting of outstanding architects, designers, engineers, planners, project managers and business consultants. After practicing as an architect in Hong Kong, Eric Shing, who was born in 1967, founded the studio in 1993. From conceptual design and architectural detailed drawing, to interior and landscape design, Shing & Partners is one of the few firms that act as a generalist. The office has been involved in more than 2,200 projects in 60 cities and towns and has been credited by more than 160 awards.

a

b

c

d

The Landmark

Location
98 Huacheng Avenue, Zhujiang New Town, Guangzhou, China
Building type residential
Completion 2017
Client Top-east Investment Group
Gross floor area 96,000 m^2

a

b

The Landmark is a high-rise architecture with an organic form that offers ultimate living experience in the city core. The 198-meter high tower is inspired by the spiral upward movement of plants. Besides its tribute on cultural context, the shape corresponds to the double arc form of Canton Tower and the Pearl River. Such a unique layout was formed by combining three towers into one, and each of them delivers different perspectives, introducing landscapes and city views into the interior. To maximize the panoramic view, the tower was rotated 27 degrees. This decision allows the building to become an extension of the central park, further reducing conflicts with the existing urban fabric. The Landmark breaks with traditional notions of residential buildings and becomes a symbol of the city with its excellent balance in technicality and aesthetics. It is this unconventional design which raised public awareness to redevelopment of the city core. Such spotlights have brought new investment and development opportunities, and empowered young entrepreneurs to revitalize and to sustain the outcomes of urban redevelopment from bottom-up.

a Extension of Central Park
b Old and new
c The City of Guangzhou
d Entrance
e Site plan
f Elevation and sections
g Final presentation
h City night view

c

d

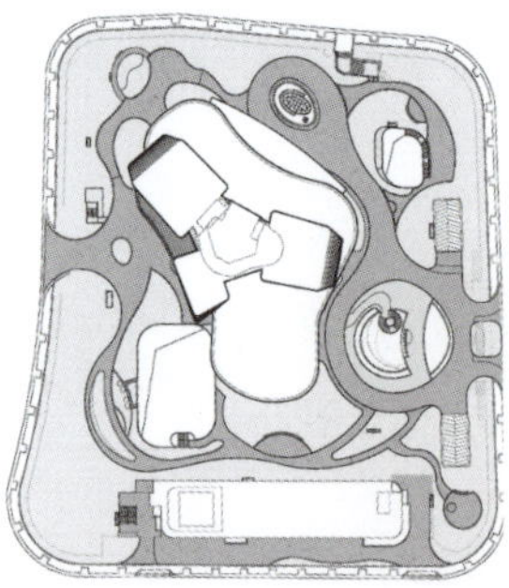

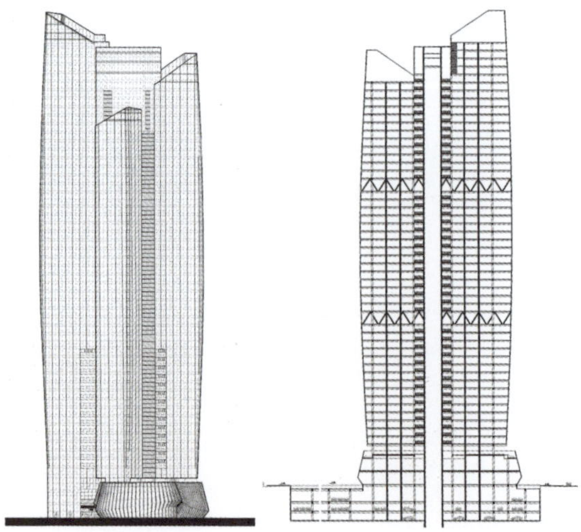

e f

g

h

CLOU architects

Jan Clostermann

Zhi Zhang, Jianyun Wu, Jan Clostermann, Lin Li, Weiming Li

a Play Stack Rotterdam
Location
Shenyang
Completion 2018

b Shoukai Vanke Center
Location
Beijing
Completion 2019

c Starry Street
Location
Chengdu
Completion 2020

The CLOU architects team designs its projects – many of them of a large scale – around community nodes and social spaces. A group of 50 talents from China and all over the world enjoys working collaboratively and imaginatively on bespoke projects. Their demanding clients range from shopping mall developers to house builders, hotel operators, and schools. In the process, CLOU architects strives to realize projects that will positively influence the people involved in its process, the environment, and the communities who live and work there. Led by German architect Jan Clostermann, born in 1977, CLOU was founded in 2015. His team of directors from all parts of the country pick up on local characteristics. The studio is located in Beijing, Shanghai and Hong Kong.

a

b

c

Vantone Center

Location
Jingxing Road, Yuhang District, Hangzhou, Zhejiang, China
Building type mixed-use
Completion 2019
Client Vantone
Gross floor area 99,250 m²

a

b

This center at Yuhang Future Science and Technology City merges retail, office space and SOHO apartments into one destination. It is designed to accommodate the multifaceted demands of a contemporary lifestyle. The grand-scale of the new Yuhang District needed a design solution that could respond to inevitable changes of the urban situation, and would be able to think in the near future: How could a project take a clear position along an upcoming skyline rapidly shaping? CLOU architects had to anticipate that neighboring sites will grow into high-density communities populated with high-rise towers. Thus the design challenge was to eliminate the under-used spaces and curate a more integrated sense of place. By introducing communal and functional spaces throughout the entirety of the development, it activates the lower levels and offers users an additional focal point aside from the monumental towers. The ultimate result is a more integrated design offering a holistic user experience. The finished towers – two parallel and one rotated – stretch upwards facing their focal point, while the podium anchors itself to the ground. Winding pedestrian passageways that circulate inwards are more intimate to the passers-by, and terraced patios and balconies encircle into generous gathering spaces. Being in a somewhat monotonous and repetitive neighborhood, the Vantone mixed-use complex hopes to generate some inviting spatial transitions and visual variations.

a Night aerial view
b Center extending to green belt
c External view
d Podium with unblocked views
e Level 1
f Level 2
g Level 3
h Section

c

d

e

f g

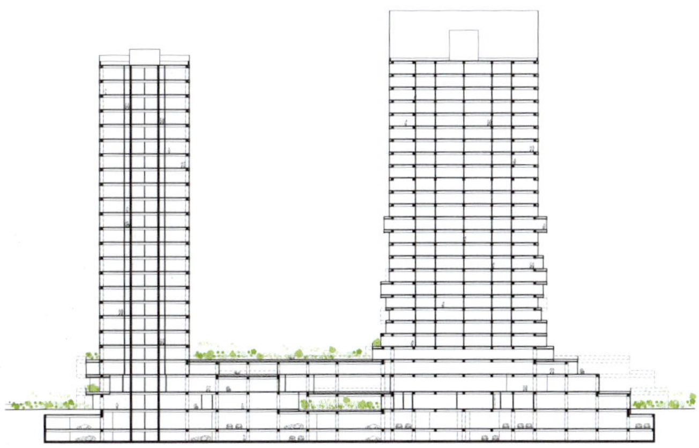

h

Atelier Alter Architects

Xiaojun Bu, Yingfan Zhang

a **Qujing Culture Center**
Location
Qujing
Completion 2015

b **Yingliang Stone Archive**
Location
Beijing
Completion 2016

c **Yingliang Stone Natural History Museum**
Location
Xiamen, Fujian
Completion 2020

d **WuliEpoch Culture Center**
Location
Beijing
Completion 2019

e **Yingliang Stone Archive**
Location
Beijing
Completion 2016

Atelier Alter Architects is based in Beijing and New York and is led by two partners – Xiaojun Bu, born 1980, and Yingfan Zhang, born 1981. Since the inception in 2009 the office has won numerous accolades. Noted for creating projects through critical analysis of the site, the works strives for transferring the physical and metaphysical context of the site into tangible yet artistic spaces of historical remembrance. Atelier Alter Architects is a cross-disciplinary practice that expends the boundary of architecture into the spatial dialogue with art, media, philosophy, and theatrical performance. On top of that, the portfolio ranges from small-scale furniture design to culture, civic, institutional projects as well as large-scale urban design. The architects try to manifest ideas of significance – ideas that offer critics rather than imitations.

a

b

c

d

e

Location
Fangshan District,
Beijing, China
Building type sports facility
Completion 2019
Client Beijing Institute of Technology
Gross floor area 15,692 m²

BIT Sports Center

a

b

The BIT Sports Center, along with the BIT Stadium, frame an entrance to the extended exurb BIT campus. The project responses to the horizontality of the site with the panoramic landscape of Yan-Shan mountain chain as the background. The project bases its tectonic on amplitude and trajectory projection – the major study areas of BIT – to stretch its formal expression on a flat site, allowing the free flow of people and thought beneath it. Besides, the parametric expression of the project also addresses the historic context of Beijing by reinstating the grayish monolithic tone in the materiality of Hutong and Great-wall. The project encompasses a basketball hall with 3,000 seats, a ten-lanes swimming pool, and spaces for martial art, taekwondo, table tennis and more. As the building form is kept simple and compact for the climate, the challenge lies in revolutionizing big-box typology from within: The humanistic landscape is created through crafting the programmatic and spatial complexity of the interior rather than the exterior. With Ludwig Mies van der Rohe's Universal Space and Cedric Price's Fun Palace in mind, the project creates an open field of porous campus that encourages visual and physical access to abundant activities. Communal space with various scales and flexible spatial definitions is thus created for new forms of networking, gathering and group activities.

a Building in landscape
b Cantilevering roof
c Main entrance
d Main lobby
e View of lobby to main entrance
f Roof structure diagram
g Roof sketch

c

d

e

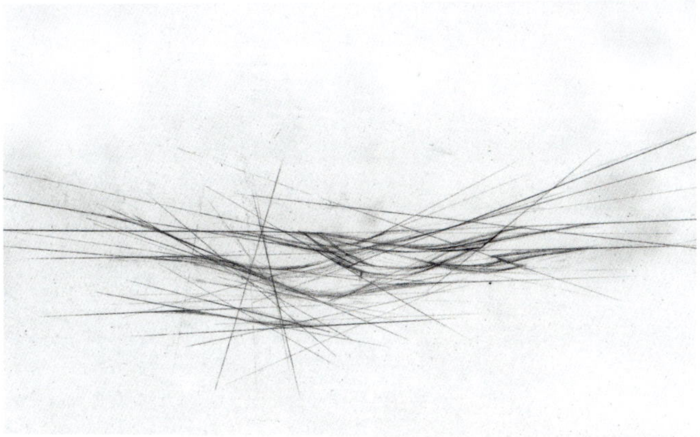

f

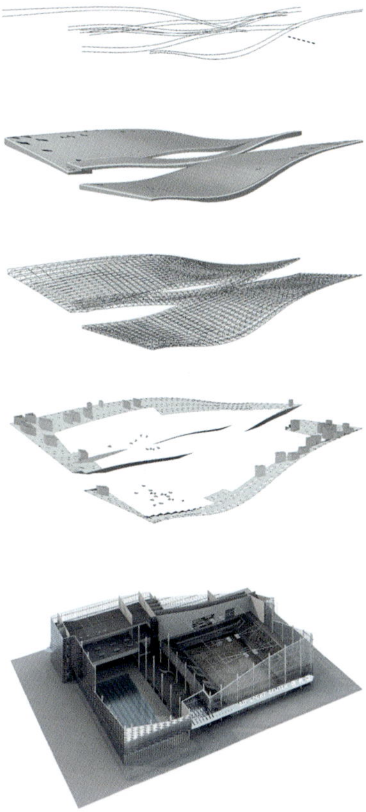

g

Crossboundaries

Binke Lenhardt, Hao Dong

a **Aimer Fashion Factory**
Location
Beijing
Completion 2014

b **Beida Affiliated Highschool**
Location
Beijing
Completion 2016

c **Chaoyang Future School**
Location
Beijing
Completion 2017

d **Soyoo Joyful Growth Center**
Location
Zhengzhou
Completion 2015

Crossboundaries is a multidisciplinary, design-centered practice with projects ranging from urban planning, architecture and interior design all the way to graphic design, programming, teaching and event creation, crossing the boundaries of the design domain and initiating activities and dialogues across different fields. The office was founded in 2005 by Binke Lenhardt, born in 1971, and Hao Dong, born in 1973. Today the Beijing office counts around 20 staff members. The Frankfurt office was founded in 2012 and is set up as a partnership with architect Antje Voigt, born in 1970. Over the years Crossboundaries has grown into an award-winning company known for its creative approach to educational projects as well as its ability to examine and expand the designated building programs generating added value for users and communities.

a

b

c

d

Beisha Village Kindergarten

Location
8 Beisha Avenue, Beisha Village, Fu'ning County, Jiangsu, China
Building type education
Completion 2018
Client Education Bureau of Fu'ning County
Gross floor area 2,815 m^2

A second home for left-behind children: The appropriate scale of the project was a crucial starting point of this design and led to a building cluster, with its required building volume broken down to house-like pieces, integrated by the central multifunctional open space. This integration of the outdoor and indoor is crucial to the early education environment and innate to the rural context. The kindergarten functions as a smaller, slightly modified version of a village, of which the scale gives children a sense of familiarity and the interesting building relationships introduce novelty and encourage curiosity. Children will first discover the overall settlement surrounded by the trees and then, as they meander in between the houses, they will experience small, secret places tucked away, perfect for outdoor learning activities and playing hide and seek, one of many games children naturally play in those small villages. So this project becomes a place where children would feel familiar and free, and with which they could identify as something like a second home. Considering that many young parents of rural areas seasonally migrate to big cities for work and miss out on big periods of their children growing up, the Beisha Village Kindergarten has a great importance to them.

a Evening view from above
b Skylit classroom
c Ground floor plan
d Playing space between the roofs
e Scale and interaction sketch
f Building cluster section

a

b

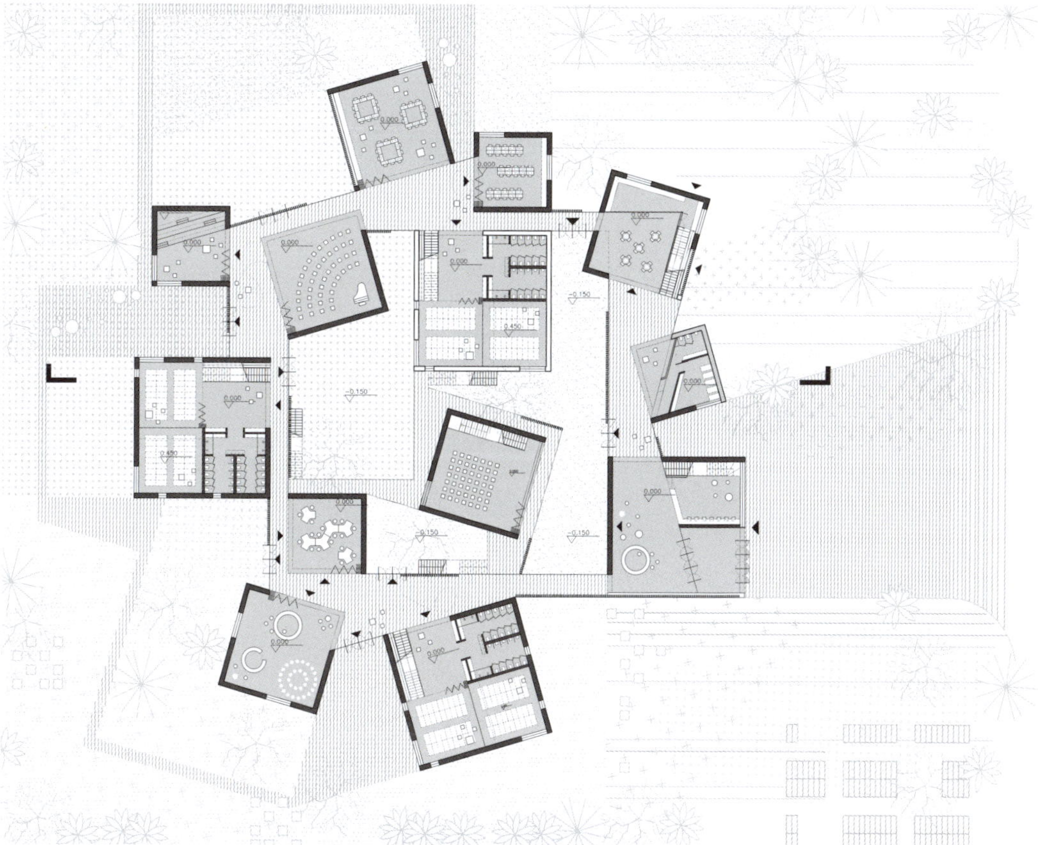

c

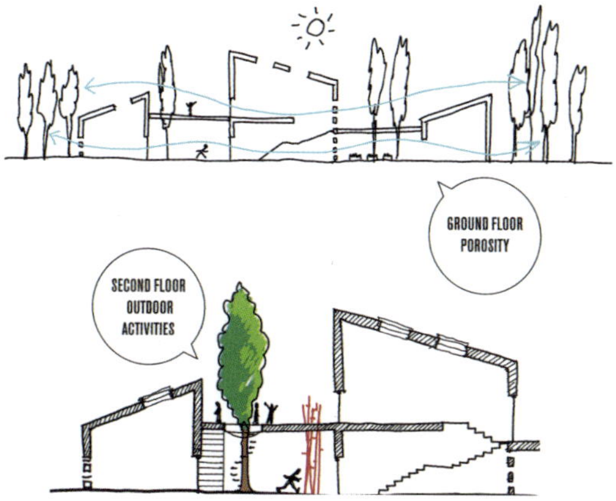

d e

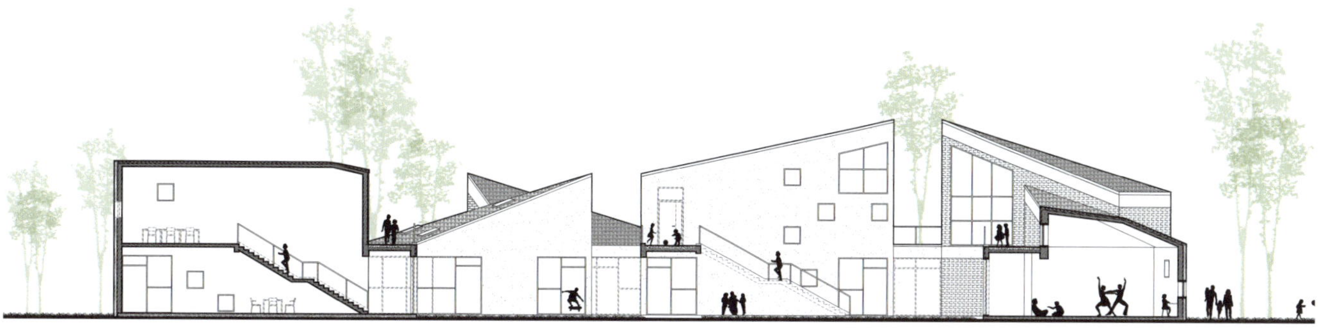

f

Sò Studio

Yifan Wu, Mengjie Liu

a SAMO Store
Location
Chonqing
Completion 2019

b CANAL ST. Selected Store
Location
Shanghai
Completion 2019

c théATRE
Location
Beijing
Completion 2019

Sò Studio is an innovative architecture, interior and industry design practice based in Shanghai. The commissions include restaurants, retail spaces, workspaces, galleries, private residences, boutique hotels and cultural institutions. The studio uses a bespoke approach for each client with applied imagination in the creative industries and intellectual rigour to create inspiring places with a powerful visual impact. Sò Studio was founded in 2016 by Yifan Wu, born in 1988, and Mengjie Liu, born in 1987, in response to the growing demand for their distinctive design aesthetic and clever use of material details in an architectural, interior and industry design context.

a

b

c

Location
F1, Taikoo Li, Sanlitun, 19
Sanlitun Road, Beijing, China
Building type commercial
Completion 2019
Client Beast
Gross floor area 245 m²

The Beast Taikoo Li Store

a

b

The façade of Beast & Little B Retail Store Taikoo Li Sanlitun Beijing is inspired by American Hard Edge artist Josef Albers. It is extracting the expressions in his work, exploring the subtle relationship between color and styling. The façade on the first floor is overall soft and tough, starting from purple to pink and finally coming to ginger yellow in the area of Little B. The building contains two sister stores with a progressive color relationship between them which distinguishes between the two sister brands. The entire façade seems like a luminous box floating in the air through its outstanding lighting. The ground floor contains the jewelry area with a pink-purple collision. Stone and metal generate a contrast, a pink spiral staircase and floral jewels create a surrounding reminding of a fairyland or dreamworld. The ground floor also includes a fireplace which was recreated with a recycled old wood fireplace. This forms a contrast between new and old. A coffee area on the first floor offers an elegant, classical and calm place with surreal elements. The style and spatial planning makes up a contrast to the one on the ground floor. The area is supposed to create a feeling of lightness for visitors who can enjoy their afternoon tea there.

a Inside shopping area
b Spiral staircase
c Coffee area
d Ground floor plan
e Part of fireplace
f Doorway leading to coffee area
g Fireplace recreation sketch
h Yellow light on outer façade
i First floor plan

c

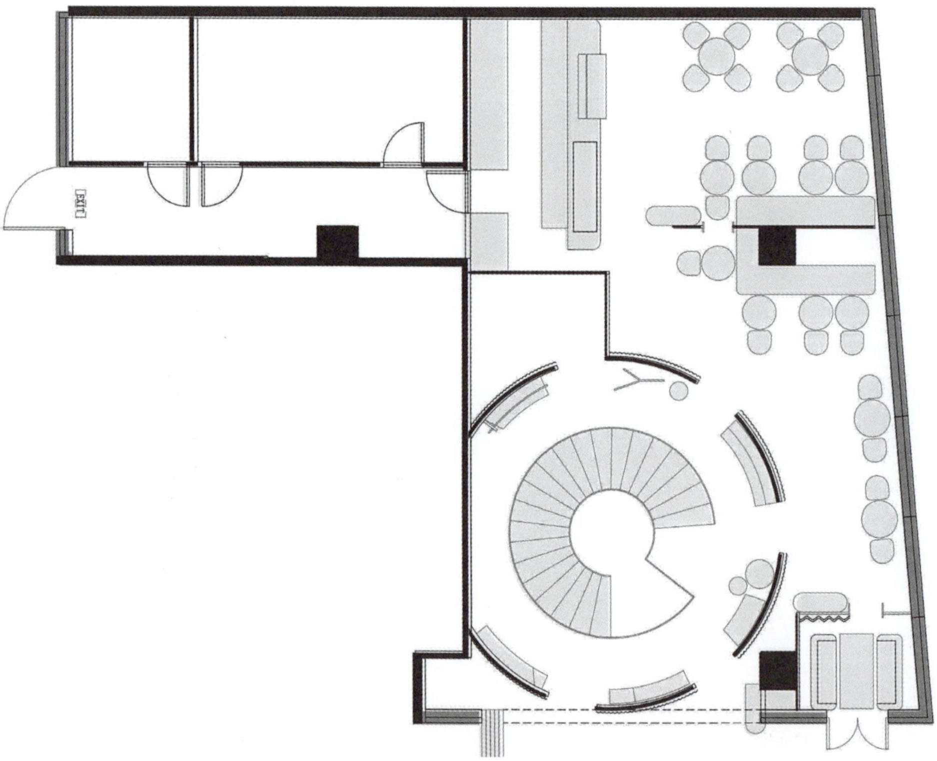

d

e f

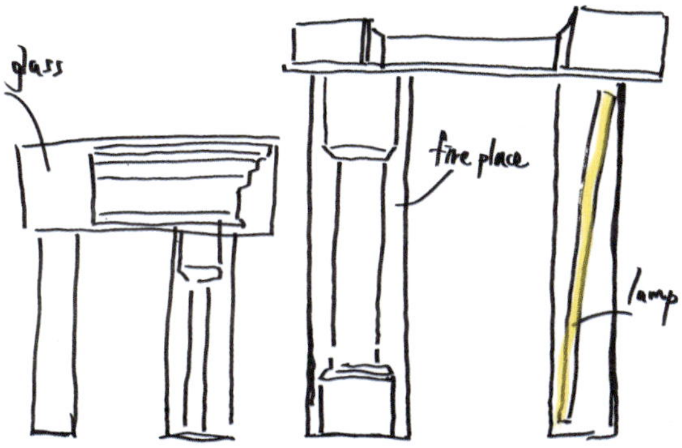

g h

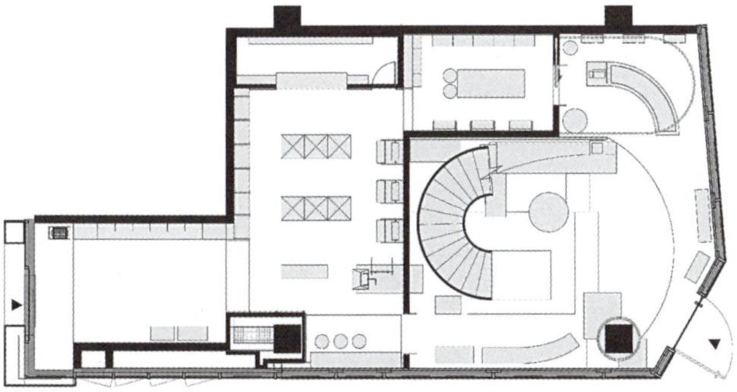

i

U10 Atelier CADG

Haiwei Yu

a China Merchants Bank
Location
Shenzhen
Completion 2017

b Film Academy
Huairou Campus
Location
Beijing
Completion 2020

c Visitor Center
Location
Yumen Pass
Completion 2018

U10 Atelier CADG was founded in 2007 by Haiwei Yu, born 1973, and is currently led by three senior architects, employing seven National Registered Architects (PRC). The office explores and challenges interesting projects, taking public building as main practice works. In addition there are office, media and exhibition buildings, skyscrapers and other typologies. The architects insist on original design, emphasize particular analysis based on different context, and are foremost interested in making architecture which will positively impact its environment while addressing the specific needs of the residents. The studio's philosophy implies that focusing on method more than result can make every design meaningful. In the design process all kinds of techniques are used from traditional hand-working model to the parametric computer model, to combine design and construction.

a

b

c

Hulunbuir Hailar Airport Expansion

Location
Hailar, Hulunbuir, Inner Mongolia
Building type infrastructure
Completion 2018
Client Hulunbuir City Investment Group
Gross floor area 20,669 m²

a

b

Hulunbuir is well known as one of the top ten snowy cities in China with its most beautiful prairies in the world. The existing airport Terminal 1 was not able to meet the need of ever-growing passenger volume for prairie tourism. For the expansion of T2 an innovative architectural form was produced - frame columns support the huge roof on the second floor by several double-V-shaped diagonal structures. The boundary between vertical and horizontal is eliminated by the structural integration of columns, ceiling and roof, to create a continuous Mongolian-yurt-like space. This golden and white huge space also makes people feel like they are in the sunny birch forest. An under-eave space with double-height is created on the land side system by the altitude difference designed between the south and north façades. Clouds and herds, the typical local elements, are beautifully expressed by the elegantly curved roof with bi-directional single-layer reticulated shells. The stretching canopy connects the new and old terminals, giving both an unified architectural language. Also, the space connectivity is achieved between the front driveways and rear waiting spaces in the two buildings, creating a pleasant under-eave space. Haiwei Yu and Yanyan Liu were the leading architects, Zhefu Jin, Yan Lu, Chao Gao and Fan He project architects. The interior was designed by Beijing Xindisen Construction Decoration Engineering Design, the lighting by Zhang Xin Studio.

a Curbside view
b Platform
c Land side aerial view
d North elevation at night
e Land side approach
f Reception hall
g Departure lounge
h Section and roof geometry

c

d

e f

g

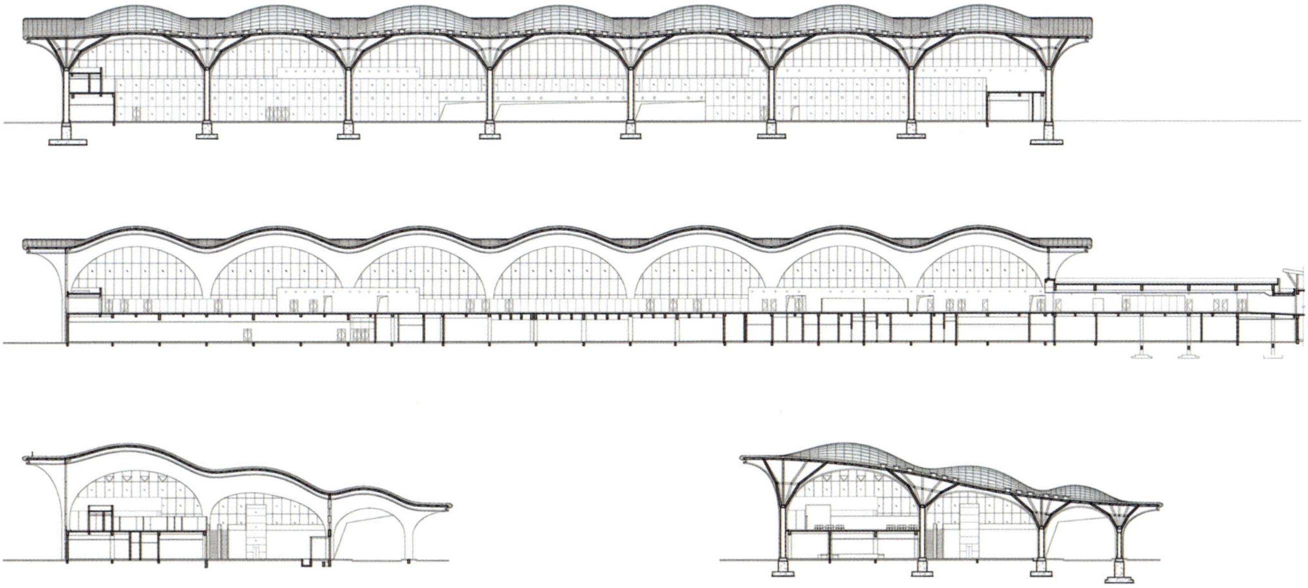

h

CU Office

Fei Che, Xuefeng Zhang

a **Dongxiang Culture Center**
Location
Maxiang
Completion 2019

b **Group of Yard House**
Location
Maxiang
Completion 2020

c **Hutong Yard**
Location
Beijing
Completion 2018

CU Office was founded in Beijing in 2007 by Fei Che, born in 1975, and Xuefeng Zhang, born in 1976. CU Office is a research and innovation-driven international integrated architectural design company. The scope of work includes architectural design, urban design and regeneration, landscape design, renovation design, interior design, and also specific types of product and exhibition design. After ten years of development, CU Office has completed a number of important research projects and development of product prototypes. The office sees its mission in the innovation of life and the interpretation of history through new spacial concepts. For the studio an integrated and clarified work method is of high value for the realization of its works and projects.

a

b

c

Location
Daliuhang, Penglai, Yantai
265615, Shangdong, China
Building type culture
Completion 2012
Client confidential
Gross floor area 1,000 m²

Villa Jian Art Museum

a

b

The concept of Villa Jian Art Museum came from the Chinese local architecture term called Jian. In local architecture culture, Jian was commonly used as a building space base unit. One Jian represented a width of about 3.3 to 3.6 meters of spatial scale and was also strongly linked with the local traditional form of construction. The client gave the condition of designing a big house with a double-slope roof covering 11 Jian. According to the needs of the client, the building should consist of two basic functions: office space and exhibition space, both limited to a semi-open private property. The exhibition space and the office were both divided into two parts: public exhibition and private exhibition, public office and private office. Public exhibition and office space were placed on the ground floor, and the private exhibition and private office were placed on the second floor. Wide stair steps were designed for seating where the semi-open exhibition space and the semi-closed office space have dramatically been intersected together. A mixed space system linking different regular functions is the core concept of the building which mainly consists of granite, concrete and glass. Bright colors and big window fronts create a welcoming light-flooded space.

a South façade
b Thinking space
c Side view detail plan
d Master plan
e Section side view
f Bright corridor
g Gallery with windows
h Exhibition hall with artworks
i View outside through windows

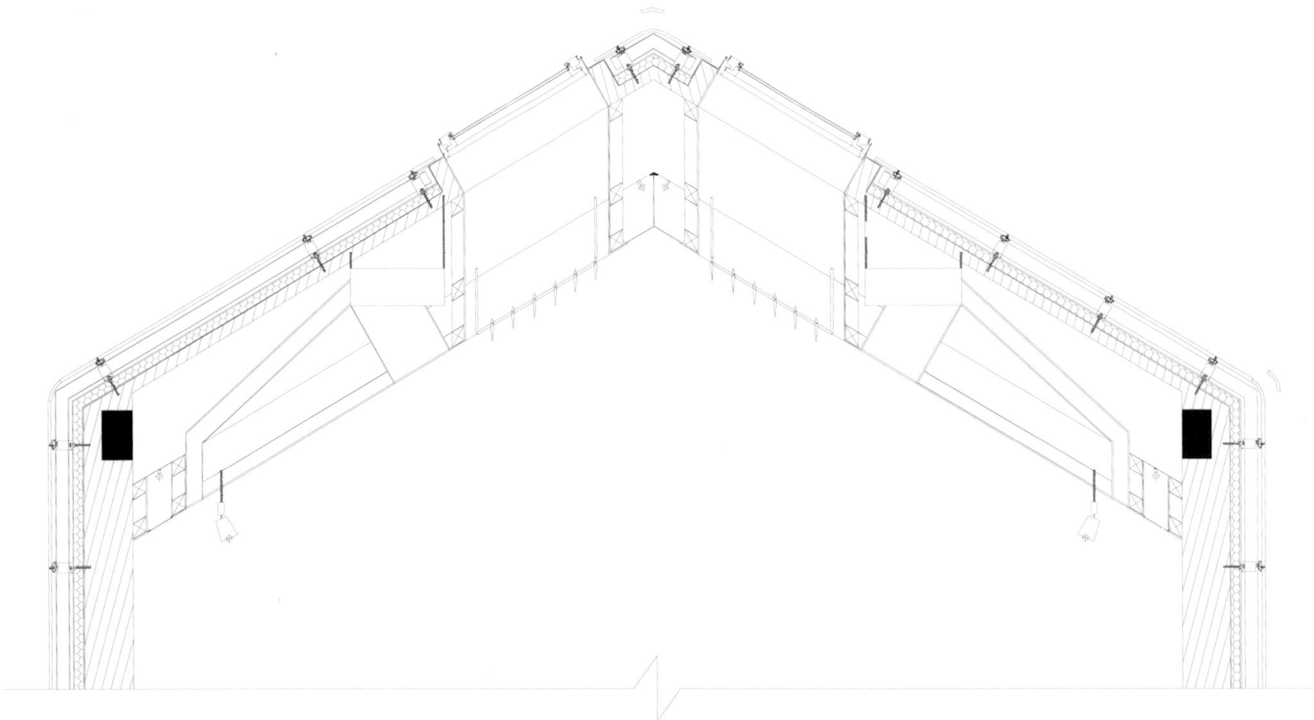

c

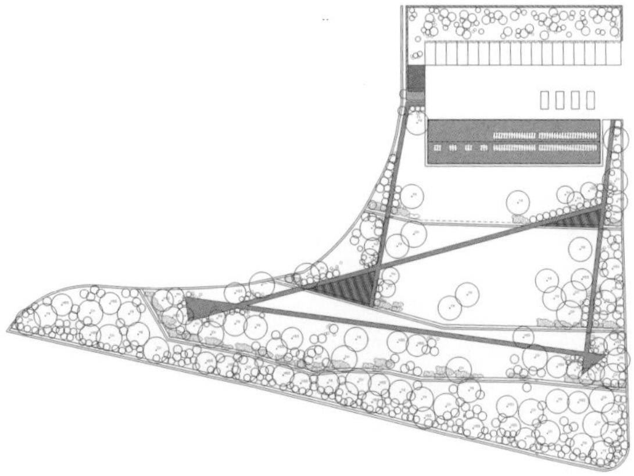

d

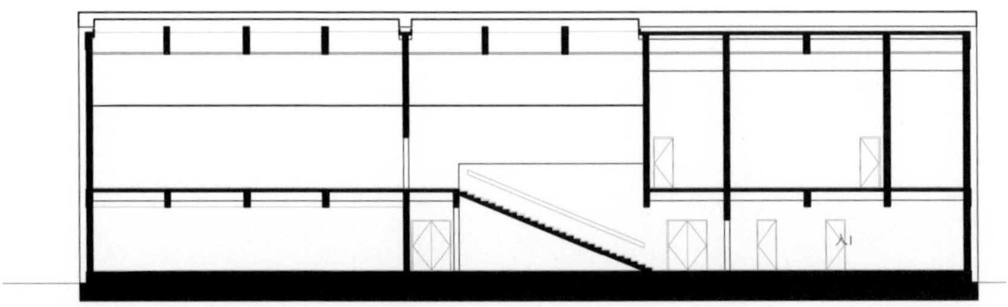

e

f g

h

i

Superimpose Architecture

Carolyn Leung

Ben de Lange

Ruben Bergambagt

a **Micr-O**
Location
Tai Yang Valley, Sun Commune, Lin'an, Hangzhou
Completion 2016

b **Micr-O**
Location
Tai Yang Valley, Sun Commune, Lin'an, Hangzhou
Completion 2016

c **Y-Loft City**
Location
Changzhi
Completion 2021

d **The Re-Veil**
Location
Changzhi
Completion 2018

e **The Re-Veil**
Location
Changzhi
Completion 2018

This studio was founded in 2016 by Carolyn Leung, born in 1984, Ben de Lange, born in 1984, and Ruben Bergambagt, born in 1983. Based in Hong Kong, Beijing and Shanghai the focus lies on applying problem-solving tactics to visible or invisible complexities of the physical world resulting in strategic, well-balanced and bold design solutions in architecture, urban planning, interior and installation design. The word Superimpose reflects their design methodology and philosophy, collaborative attitude, team structure and knowledge-sharing mentality: Place one thing over another as an addition, in such a way that all layers are still evident. This means collaboration with related disciplines like sustainability experts, artists, or craftsmen. It demands contextual awareness with the responsibility to improve, protect, recycle and sustain both our natural and built environments.

a

b

c

d

e

CO2 Pavilion

Location

Yan Jing Lane, Chaoyang District, Beijing, China

Building type culture

Completion 2018

Client Shard Island

Gross floor area 15 m^2

The CO2 Pavilion was designed for the Beijing Design Week 2018 as an enclosed place for isolation and contemplation from urban chaos, and as a three-dimensional projection screen for multidisciplinary performances on the multilayered exterior. Ultimately architecture, music, visual art and light art work hand in hand to consolidate awareness about the conditions of the cities people inhabit. It strives to restore the missing sense of gathering and togetherness rooted in the traditional Chinese siheyuan way of living. The CO2 pavilion is a horizontal volume of light and smoke in the center of a grey brick courtyard. It is composed of 26 square-sectioned frames tied together through the simple use of bolts and nuts in a system of three different modules that encloses a portion of open space into an inner patio open to the sky. During the Beijing Design Week, the pavilion became the physical backdrop for a series of public events and workshops curated by the creative studio Shard Island who invited artists from different backgrounds to share their stories. Catwalk shows, guzheng (a Chinese harp) and piano play, artificial intelligence performances and digital art projections all superimpose to a holistic piece of art.

a Non-toxic theatrical steam
b First tree
c Floor plan
d Courtyard within courtyard
e Section
f Second tree

a b

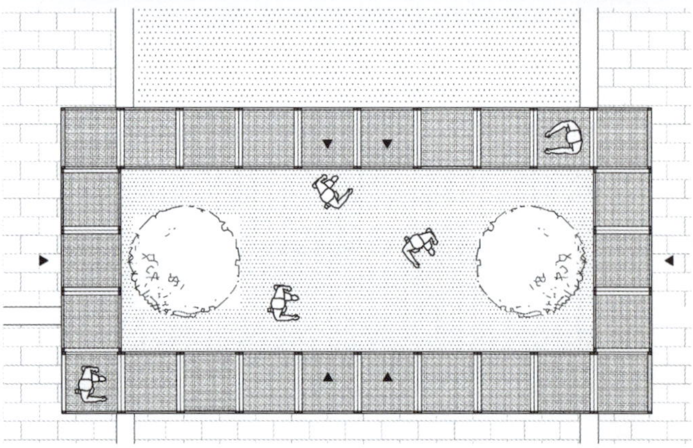

c d

e

HHDFUN

Zhenfei Wang, Luming Wang

a **Shiyu Headquarters**
Location
Beijing
Completion 2018

b **The Bar**
Location
Nanning
Completion 2019

c **Yuan Xiang Hotel**
Location
Tianjin
Completion 2018

d **The Coral**
Location
Beijing
Completion 2018

e **The T**
Location
Tianjin
Completion 2017

HHDFUN is a design and research studio, which consists of architects, designers, programmers and more. With interests in bringing knowledge from various fields outside of architecture and applying them into architecture design, the studio devotes itself to the production of unexpected and extraordinary designs which distinguish from the conventional. The studio was founded in 2009 by Zhenfei Wang, born in 1977, and Luming Wang, born in 1980. HHDFUN is cooperating with people from all walks of life, such as artists, fashion designers, mathematicians and engineers. Together those different kind of people are exploring the new design possibilities by means of this cross-over cooperation through different approaches and ways of thinking.

a

b

c

d

e

Dichi Service Center

Location International Horticultural Exposition, Tianshui Road, Licang District, Qingdao, China
Building type mixed-use
Completion 2014
Client 2014 Qingdao International Horticultural Exposition
Gross floor area 9,600 m²

a

b

The Dichi Service Center was part of the International Horticultural Exposition 2014. It is located on the Baiguo Mountain and was built for different functions such as a circulation hub, an activity center, a restaurant, a place for cultural communication, and exhibition. For the realization of the project three key elements were being followed and kept in mind: Reasonable use of differences in natural gradient was seen as particularly important. The architecture and landscape heights are set following the natural grade levels, providing multiple accessibilities and viewing experiences at different elevations. The main architecture spaces are lower than the surrounding street levels, facing the central sunken courtyard, thereby accommodating the visitors while affording view of preeminent water landscape. Secondly the preservation of the extant landscape and vegetation to the greatest extent had an important part for the construction process. All the trees in the area were preserved in their entirety and a rooftop platform promotes a building efficiency and integration of the architecture into the landscape. Lastly a multi-trail system played a huge role for the design. A three-dimensional diamond-shaped grid system was used for it. This then carried out self-adaptive adjustment according to the variations in land form and functional needs, forming a series of sequential spatial systems at various heights.

a Aerial view
b Detail
c Position plan
d Sunken plaza
e Surrounding landscape
f Principle plan

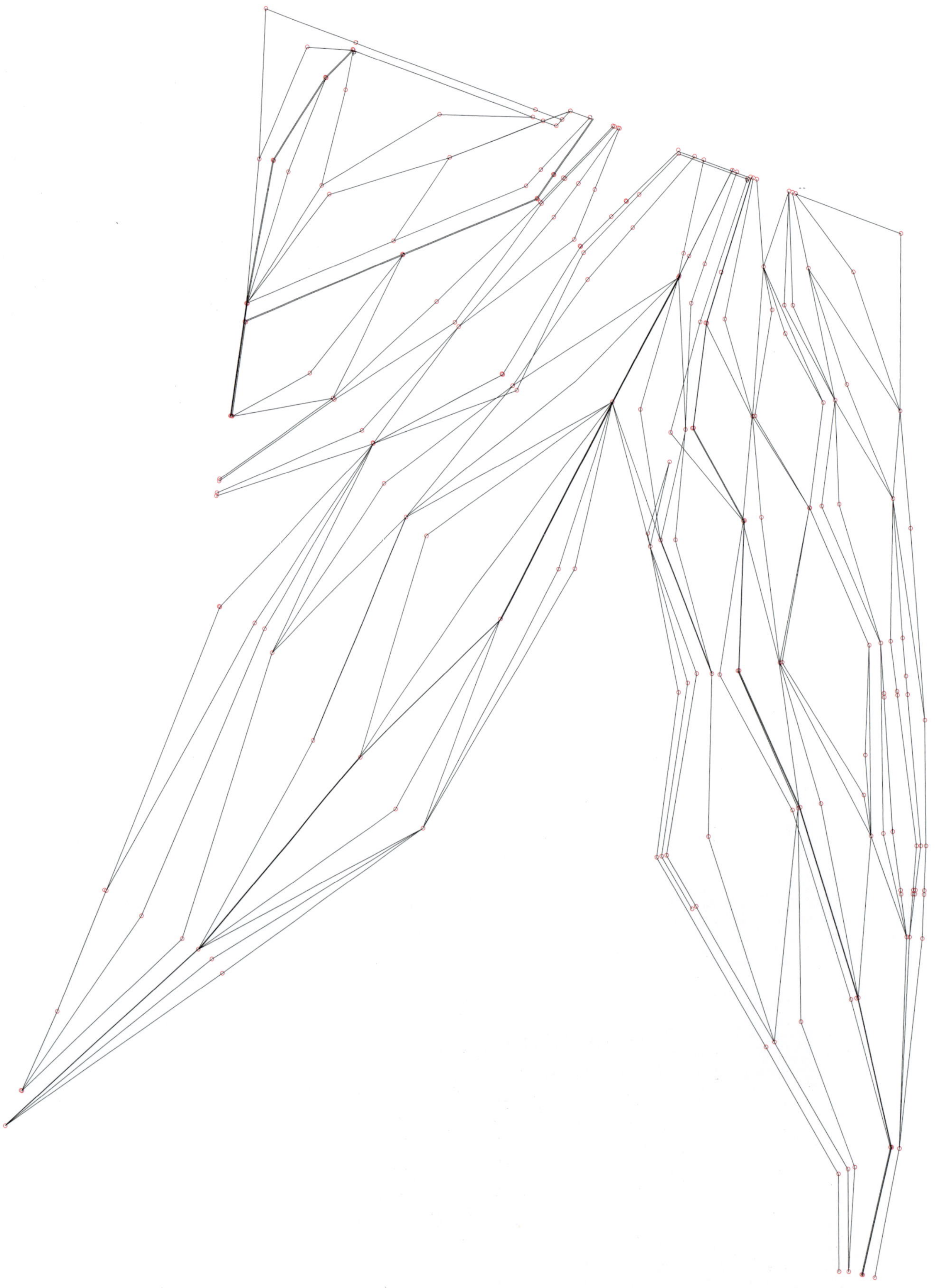

c

d

e

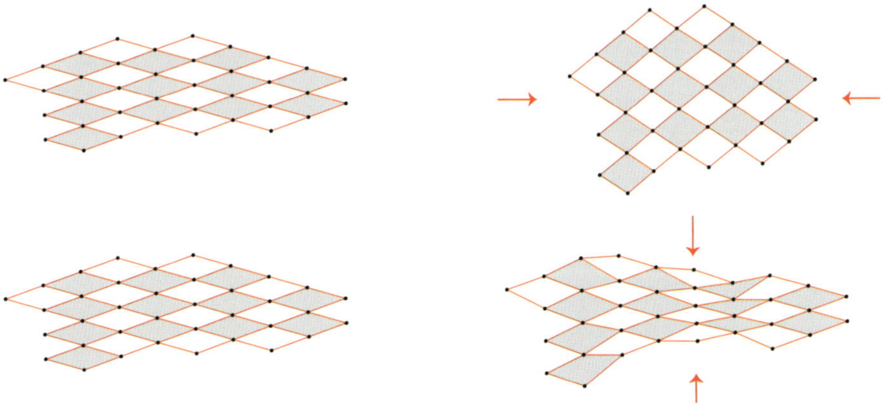

f

Scenic Architecture Office

Xiaofeng Zhu

a Dongyuan Community Center
Location
Suzhou
Completion 2017

b Activity Homes at Yunjin Road
Location
Shanghai
Completion 2018

c Gao'an Road No. 1 Primary School Huazhan Campus
Location
Shanghai
Completion 2020

d Lattice Book House
Location
Shanghai
Completion 2016

Scenic Architecture Office was founded in 2004 in Shanghai by Xiaofeng Zhu who was born in 1972. The studio initiates its works from the needs of body and mind, nature and society and tries to establish a balanced and dynamic relationship between these needs through ontological orders composed by space, time and tectonics. In recent years of practice, it has been focusing on exploring the potential of clustered space and form in the present to carve a new identity for contemporary Chinese architecture niched between tradition and the future. The works of Scenic Architecture Office have been widely published by both international and local media, and the office has been invited to participate in various international architectural exhibitions. Many projects of the studio have been awarded in both home ground and abroad with awards like the Archdaily Annual China Architecture Award.

a

b

c

d

Shanghai Google Creators' Society Center

Location
404 Guling Road,
Shanghai 200233, China
Building type corporate
Completion 2013
Client
China Fortune Properties
Gross floor area 730 m²

a

b

The location of the Shanghai Google Creators' Society Center at downtown Shanghai is a green thoroughfare with six aged camphor trees. The landscape design was created by DLC Landscape. The design boasts two main strategies: elevate the main volume to the first floor to maximize the open ground space, and protect the trees on the site to establish an intimate and interactive relationship with them. Four suspended structures, linked to one another by bridges, are supported by ten pieces of reinforced-concrete walls. The walls are cleverly camouflaged in reflective, stainless-steel panels to reflect the surrounding green environment, making them practically disappear. The four floating volumes weave in between the old camphor trees, and are wrapped by translucent twisted-strip aluminum skin. Visitors will encounter courtyards, bridges, and trees in the maze of these translucent walls. The collaboration between architecture and nature fosters interaction of nature, tectonics, time and space.

a Water courtyard side view
b Bridge connects the construction
c Bridge leading indoor
d Front view of courtyard
e Section
f Tea house at first floor
g Tree surrounded by construction
h Ground floor space

c

d

e

f g

h

MTMdesign

Max Trullás

Fanghai

a **The Battery NY Eatery**
Location
Shanghai
Completion 2019

b **Bandido Tacos & Tequila**
Location
Ho Chi Minh City, Vietnam
Completion 2019

c **High Yaki**
Location
Shanghai
Completion 2020

d **Tomatito @Xintiandi**
Location
Shanghai
Completion 2019

MTMdesign is an interior design studio founded in 2013 by architect Max Trullás Moreno from Barcelona. He was born in 1981 and arrived in Shanghai in 2008, after getting his degree at the ETSAV Barcelona Tech. His office located in Shanghai is specialized in Food & Beverage and hospitality projects. The office is also directed by Fanghai, born in 1980. MTMdesign has experience in multiple Asian markets like China, the Philippines, Hong Kong (China), Korea, Indonesia and Vietnam. Typical of MTMdesign is that they craft every project as a unique story. Each context, location, concept and client deserves a unique narrative as an answer to his needs. The office engages with the final user, creating comfortable environments and emotional experiences with a fun twist. Max Trullás' design philosophy is that life is too short to dine or work in a boring space.

a

b

c

d

Heritage by Madison

Location
1/F, 600 Zhongshan Dong Er Lu, Shanghai, China
Building type hospitality
Completion 2019
Client Madison Group
Gross floor area 350 m²

a

b

MTMdesign created Heritage by Madison together with Studio Illumine functioning as lighting consultant. The project reflects and celebrates chef Austin Hu's mix of cultures. NYC lofts were taken as a starting point of the design: Their openness, industriality, high ceilings have been reformulated in an refined Asian language. The material palette consists of textured glass brick, brass plated stainless steel, woven brass mesh, and wood. The main feature at the so called kitchen room is its 20-meter-long counter with its bespoke chandelier. It connects the cocktail bar with the open kitchen, changing its height with a raise of the platform creating different seating experiences. It is the gathering point and serves as theatrical stand to interact with chefs and mixologists. The services block is dematerialized with a programmable backlit textured glass brick skin that functions as a glowing lantern. Warm colored light enhances the sense of liveliness at dinner time. Cool blues and turquoises in the late evenings, however, evoke a sense of mystery and sophistication when the restaurant turns into a bar. Separated by sliding panels – that look like rattan made of brass – sits the library lounge. Flanked with floor-to-ceiling bookshelves and artwork, the lounge serves to be a more private and relaxed space. The bespoke brass domes on walls and ceiling help to create an intimate and cozy environment.

a Bar counter with color scene
b Dining lounge
c Open-kitchen dining counter
d Dining room and open kitchen
e Dining lounge
f Layout plan

c

d

e

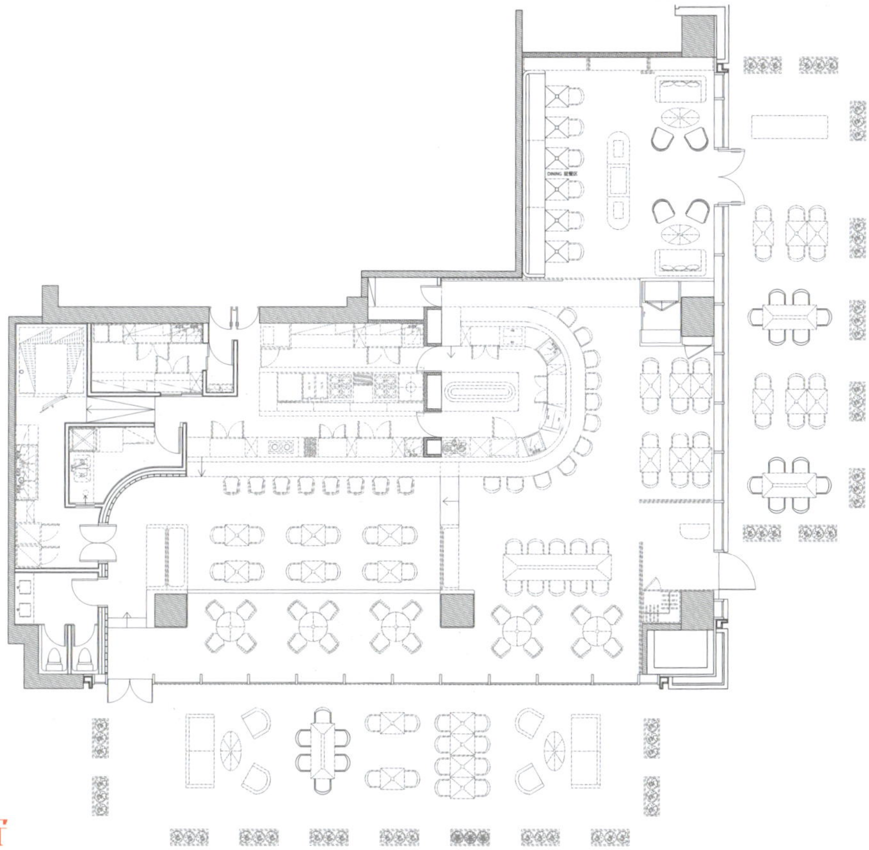

f

Atelier DYJG

Qing Lin Xiangrong Wang

a Jiangyangfan Ecopark
Location
Hangzhou
Completion 2010

b Four Boxes Garden
Location
Xi'an
Completion 2011

c Jinquan River Waterfront Park
Location
Jinan
Completion 2019

d Yunyang Riverside Green Corridor
Location
Chongqing
Completion 2018

Xiangrong Wang, born in 1963, and Qing Lin, born in 1971, founded the landscape planning and design firm Atelier DYJG in Beijing in 2000. Atelier DYJG covers a wide range of fields and has completed a lot of exploratory projects. The office aims at the specific goal regarding each site by recognizing its problems and searching for the most reasonable solutions. Every project seeks for the best balance among nature, society, art, ecology, technology, economy and other factors. Atelier DYJG has completed more than 100 projects in 20 years of practice, covering for example regional landscape planning, green infrastructure planning, urban design, parks, wetlands and gardens. Many of its projects are among the most significant and influential landscape projects in China. The studio has won several awards like the ASLA Professional Award for its works.

a

b

c

d

Quarry Gardens

Location 20 Puxing Avenue, Nanning 530200, China
Building type recreational
Completion 2018
Client Organizing Committee of Nanning Garden Expo
Gross floor area 350,000 m²

a

b

c

As part of the international garden Expo seven quarries were transformed into distinctive gardens. To cope with this complex project, UAV aerial scanning – Unmanned Aerial Vehicles laser scanning – was adopted to acquire 3D terrain data of the site. Continuous observation and record were also executed for hydrological data of stone pits' water variations. Distinguishing restoration methods and intervention approaches were adopted according to various scales, the space structure, and characteristics of these quarries. The towering cliffs, fragmented rocks, bottomless pools, stacked soil, slag stones, and rusty quarrying machinery are all regarded as landscape resources to be integrated into the design. Space shaping, vegetation restoration, paths and viewpoints were conceived on the basis of these. Eventually, the quarry gardens preserve the site's unique history and characteristics and incorporate the theme of horticulture and landscape art. They create a rich sensory experience for visitors who can walk on bridges and staircases. The project was realized together with the China Design and Research Group and the Nanning Gujin Institute responsible for the landscape design. It showcases inspiring ways for revitalizing a derelict mining site.

a Rich spatial experience
b Curved bridge above water
c Viewpoint on plant habitats
d Terrace garden plan
e Pavilion with view on cliff
f Path through aquatic plant garden
g Terrace garden digital model

d

e

f

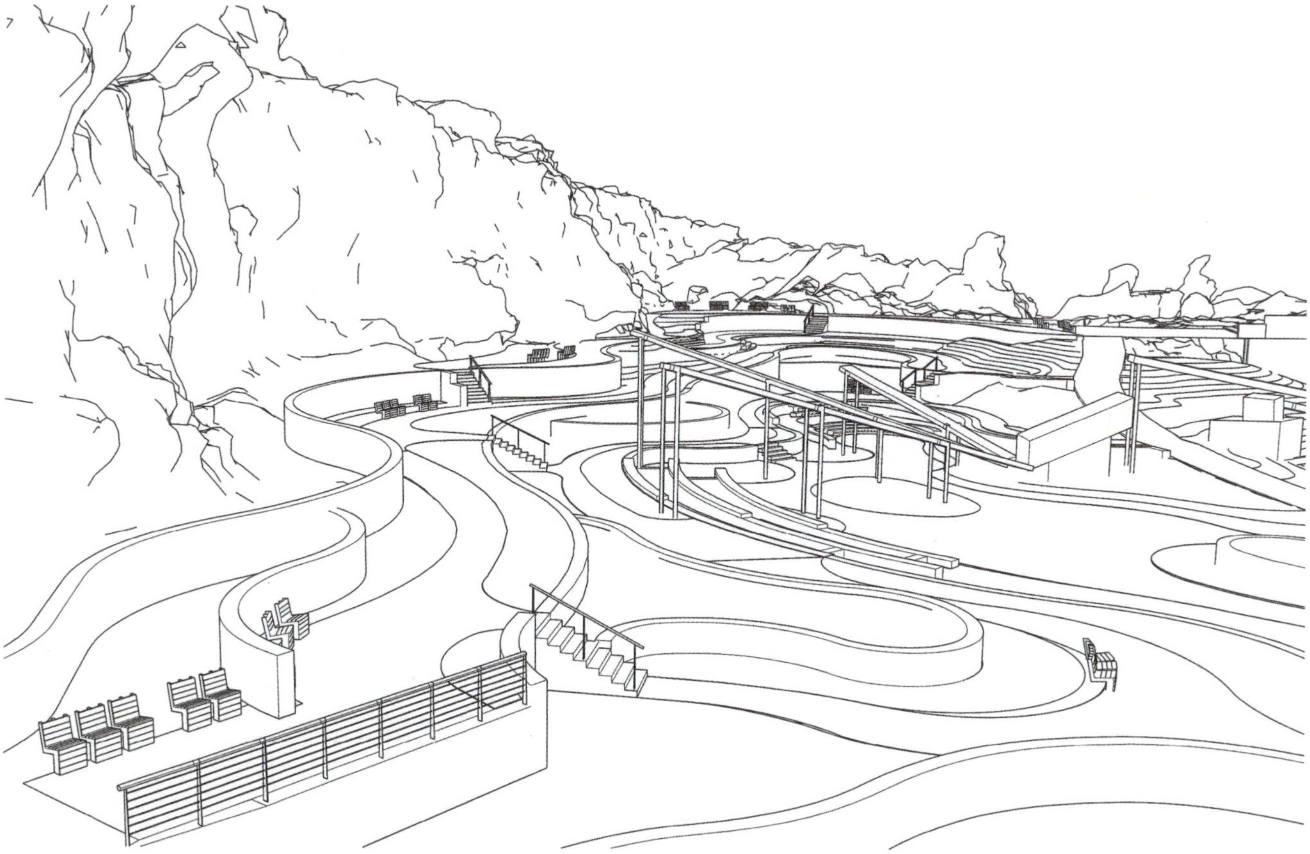

g

Luo Studio

Luo Yujie

a Party and Public Service Center of Yuanheguan Village
Location
Hubei
Completion 2019

b Natural Library in Zheshui Village
Location
Shanxi
Completion 2020

c Temporary Site of Shengli Market
Location
Henan
Completion 2019

Luo Yujie, born in 1984, is not only a teacher of construction basics in the School of Architecture at the Central Academy of Fine Arts (CAFA), he also founded the Luo Studio in 2017. Through his work with the studio he is committed to creating more durable, friendly and higher quality spaces with creative thinking, a spirit of craftsmanship and the principle of caring for nature. Therefore he for example uses the remains of abandoned buildings and natural materials for his work. Many of his projects have been successfully rewarded with several worldwide design awards. For example he has been the gold winner of the WAN Awards 2019 for the category Wood in Architecture and also won in the category Best Achievement in Environmental Performance at the ABB LEAF Awards 2019.

a

b

c

Longfu Life Experience Center

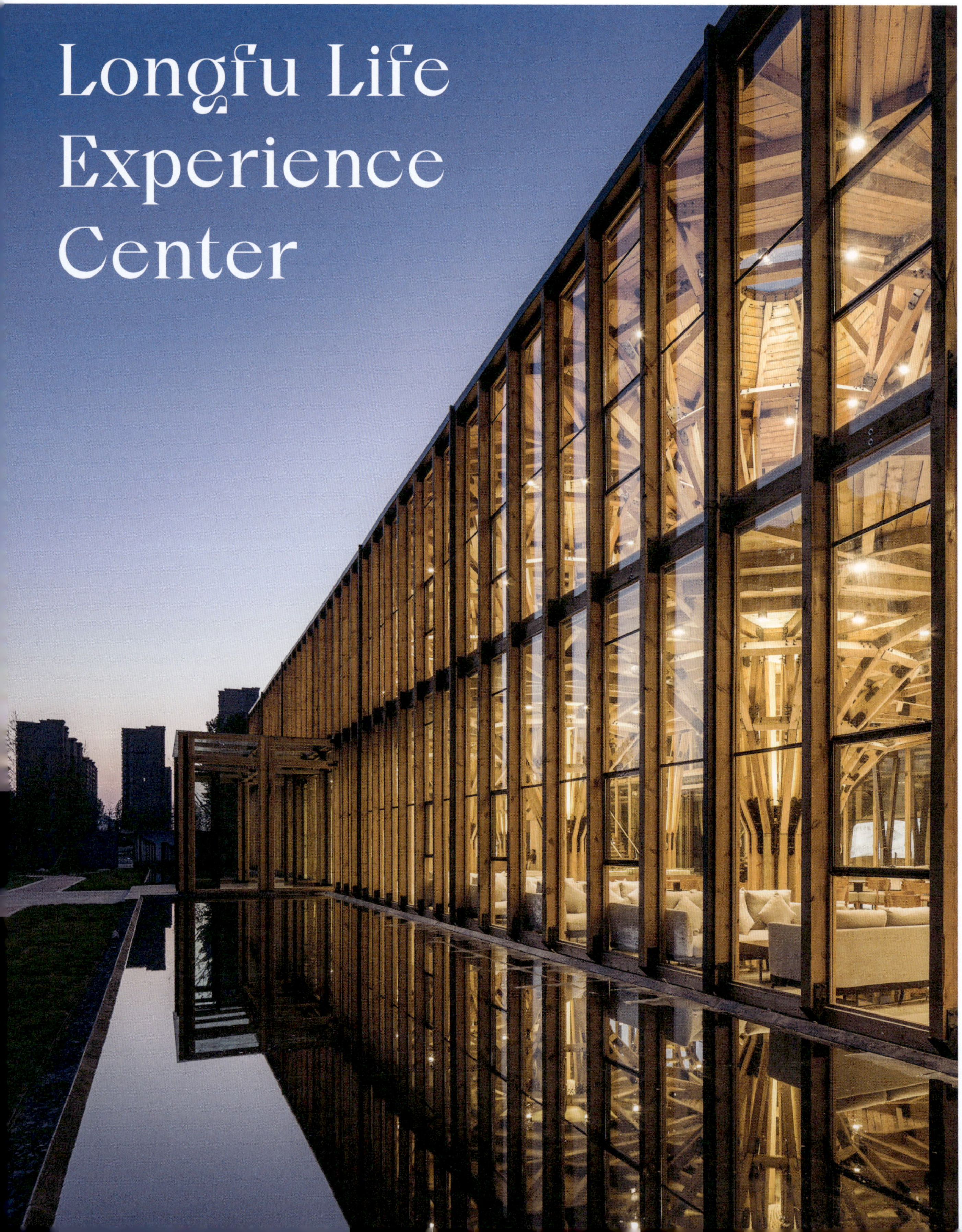

Location
Intersection Changqing Road / Fumin Road, Puyang, Henan, China
Building type commercial
Completion 2018
Client Estancerio Lai Lijun
Gross floor area 4,478.45 m²

a

b

c

Constructed on an area of 1,588 square meters, the Longfu Life Experience Center was built as a temporary real estate sales center to only last several months or a few years. The building is thoroughly reversible and seen as a universally-used space. The reusable and dismounted house was created by the use of simple and basic construction and common material processing techniques. Components can be completely dismounted, installed, moved and reused. Timbers in the form of square logs were used as a green and natural material for construction. To build a large solid space and maximize its possible functions, several square timber pillars were combined to form a clustered column. Horizontal units of these were designed in the shape of regular dodecagon. The vertical units designs were applied in the shapes of trees divided into five segments to maximize the lower and structural space. These clustered columns extend upwards from the bottom and form a square outside edge. Each unit along the edge was horizontally and longitudinally interlined and is independent or combined with others to create an extensible space. The continuous archs between the units make the overall structure very stable. Equipment, electromechanics, pipelines, furniture and exterior were integrated into those units and create a smart space resembling cavity of the human body.

a View of the outdoor area
b Green area around the building
c Illuminated exterior façade
d Outer and inner design sketch
e Continuous arches on ground floor
f Clustered columns and windows

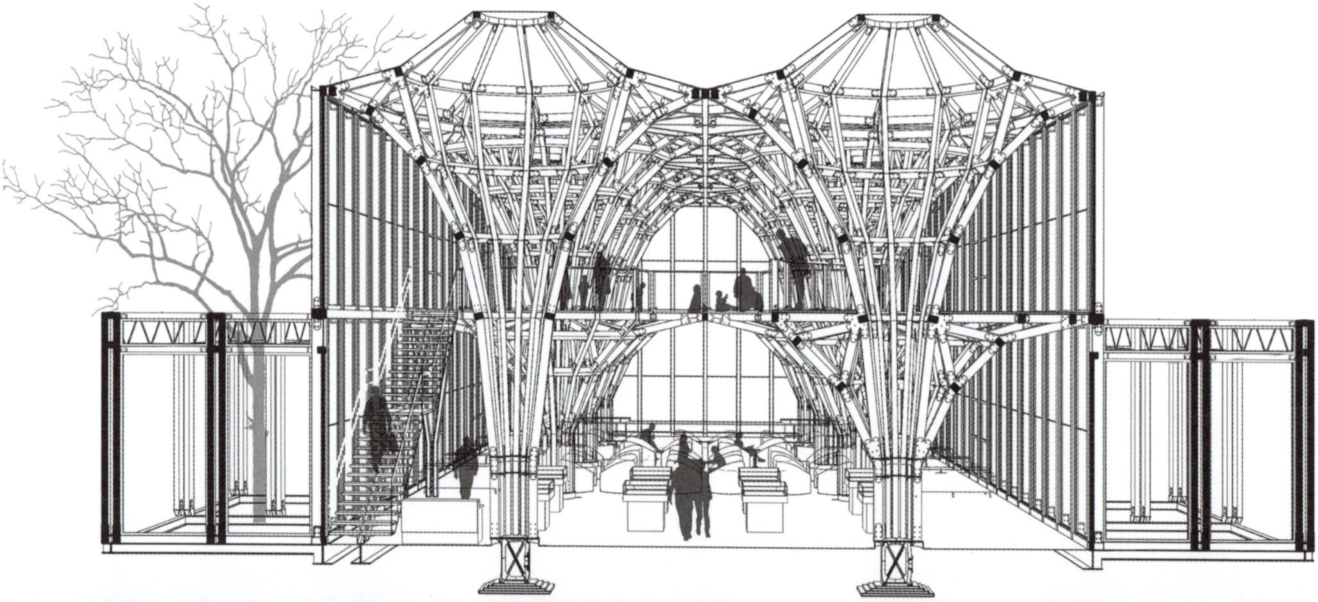

d

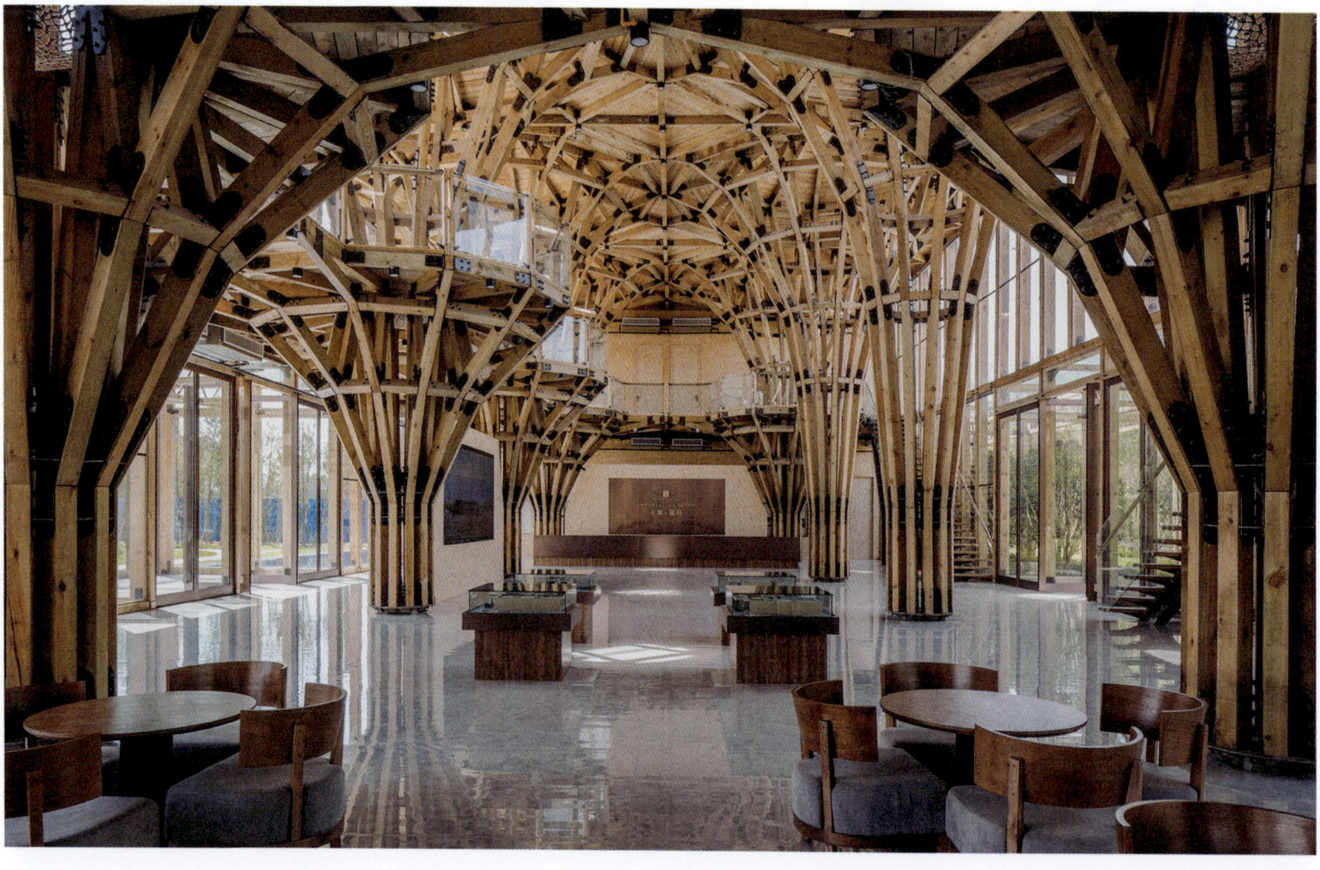

e

Miao Design Studio

Pu Miao

a **Jinguyuan Mixed-Use Complex**
Location
Kunshan
Completion 2013

b **New Jiangwan Ecological Exhibition Center**
Location
Shanghai
Completion 2005

c **Reception Center, Minhang Ecological Garden**
Location
Shanghai
Completion 2004

d **Zhuting Church**
Location
Zhuzhou
Completion 2002

e **Sichang-Road Teahouse**
Location
Kunshan
Completion 2007

Established in 1992, Miao Design Studio is headed by Dr. Pu Miao, born 1950, an architect, scholar and educator based in Shanghai, China and Honolulu, USA. His work is dedicated to the practice and theory of a modern architecture and urbanism localized in the context of China. Pu Miao's design and research focuses on the integration of architecture and landscape – a living feature of the tradition – and the creation of public spaces in high-density cities. His works have won several awards and have been published and exhibited internationally. He served as a member of the UN-Habitat Expert Group Meeting on public space. Educated at Tongji University, Shanghai (B.S.) and UC Berkeley (M.Arch., Ph.D.), Pu Miao is a Professor at the School of Architecture, University of Hawaii at Manoa.

a

b

c

d

e

Visitor Center, Xingxi Park

Location
Xingxi Park, Xincheng Road, Kunshan, China
Building type recreational
Completion 2017
Client Kunshan City Construction, Investment and Development
Gross floor area 500 m^2

A three-kilometer-long linear park lies east-west between two parallel railways in the suburb of Kunshan. For a high-density city, Xingxi Park converts a wasteland into a public space for residents to hike, bike, and boat. The visitor center utilizes concrete, steel, aluminum perforated panel, and wood. It sits at the east end of the park. An existing footbridge over a sunken street connects the site with a railway station plaza that is 4.45 meters higher than the site. To arouse visitors' interest in the park, the footbridge becomes the main entry and is extended into a roof plaza enclosed by screens. At the west end of the plaza, a semicircular gate behind a pool opens up a view of the park, suggesting an illusory path into the park. But people actually descend into the park via a wide stair sideways, a pause to induce anticipation. The ground floor contains all utilitarian functions such as a gift shop, bicycle rental and boat piers. The contrast between the two floors intends to add a spiritual experience to the building type that often overemphasizes material needs. Since the opening, many weddings have taken place in front of the gate.

a Gate view into the park
b Gate at dusk
c Stair connects the roof plaza
d Bridge to roof plaza
e Upper floor plan
f Lower floor plan

a

b

c d

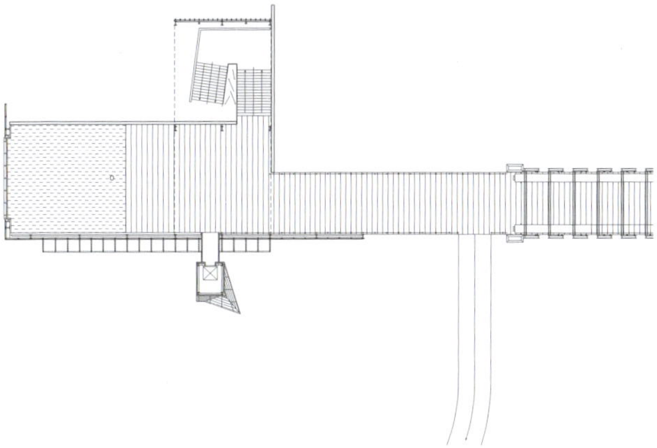

e

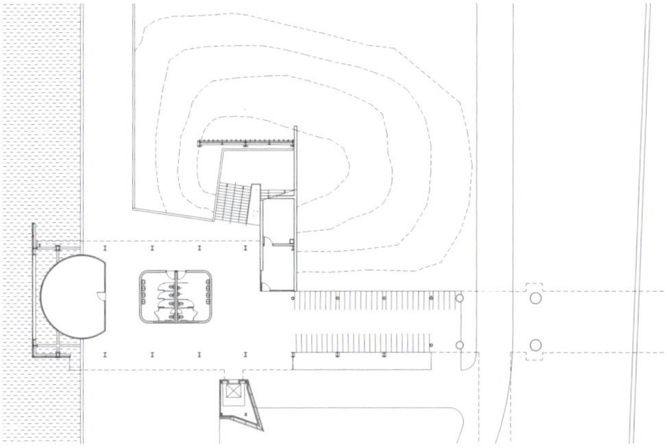

f

Group of Architects

The studio

Hao Lu

a **OōEli (JNBY & GOA Headquarters)**
Cooperation RPBW
Location
Zhejiang
Completion 2020

b **Shanghai Tao Hua Yuan**
Location
Shanghai
Completion 2019

c **Fengying Stone Art Museum**
Location
Chongwu
Completion 2018

d **Sino-Ocean International Center**
Location
Zhejiang
Completion 2017

Group of Architects, GOA, was founded in 1998 in Hangzhou and is led by Hao Lu, born in 1967. The large design organization with premium architectural quality as its mission, provides customers with integrated professional services. The company currently boasts a pool of more than 800 professionals and has set up offices in Hangzhou, Shanghai, Beijing and Nanjing. With irreplaceable pioneering advantages in fields such as luxury residences, hotels, headquarters and sci-tech parks, GOA is one of the first private design organizations that obtains the national Class A qualification in construction engineering. More than 30 principals and their teams are connected through systems including the parts of Project Manager, Design Manager and Engineering Manager. They provide systematic design solutions to customers with highly diversified and well-processed works.

a

b

c

d

Location
939 Ziye East Road, Wuzhen,
Tongxiang, Jiaxing,
Zhejiang, China
Building type hospitality
Completion 2018
Client YADA International
Gross floor area 25,000 m²

Alila Wuzhen

a

b

Alila Wuzhen, situated only three kilometers away from the well-known Xizha tourist area, is an oasis of serenity amid chaos. The modern-looking hotel includes 126 villa-type suites and is inspired by the villages south of the Yangtze River, retaining the spacial forms, basic elements, architectural scales and color relations of traditional tribes. The architects, working together with Z+T Studio for landscape design, endowed streets, lanes and courtyards with new functions and spirits by exploring the possibility of traditional space reconstruction. The design follows the minimalist aesthetic tendency of Oriental culture and the architects captured and extracted the concise, exquisite and silent aesthetic interest of buildings south of the Yangtze River. They abandoned all straight forward decorative elements, and introduced fine materials, concise structures and quietly elegant colors with modern tones. The hotel has overall completed its inheritance of local culture and the spatial prototype of villages south of the Yangtze River.

a Entrance of public area
b Courtyard space with trees
c Indoor swimming pool at sunset
d Lobby
e Aerial view by night
f Garden villa bedroom
g Preliminary sketch of master plan

c

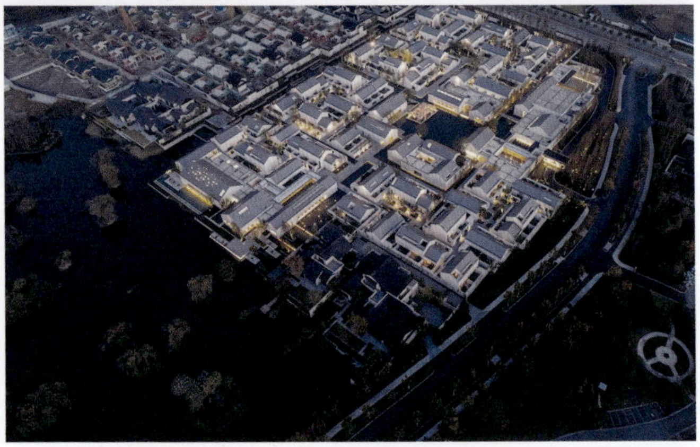

d e

f

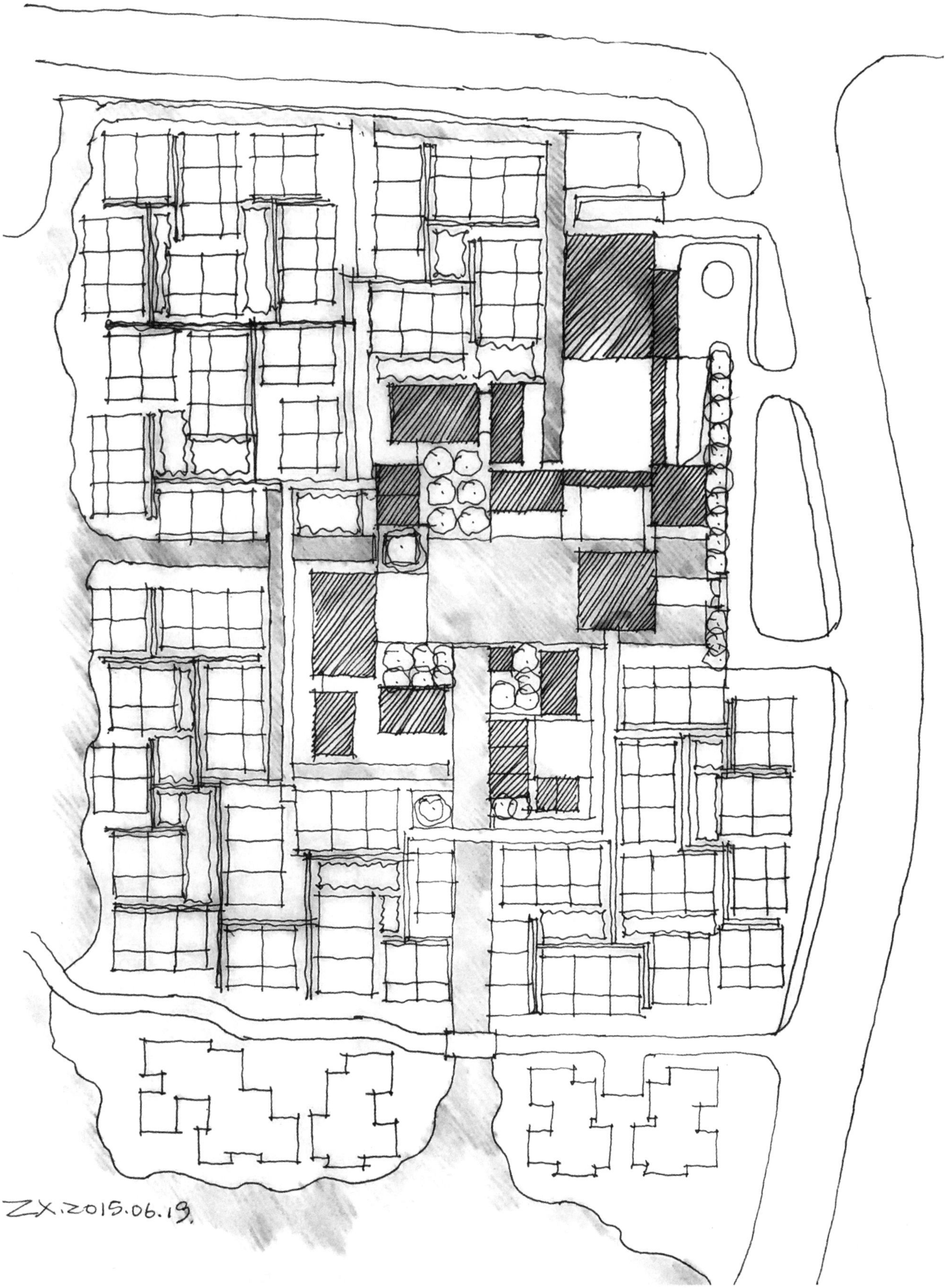
ZX.2015.06.19.

Hallucinate Design Office

Wenliang Wang

a United Imaging Booth
Location
Chicago, IL, USA
Completion 2018

b Dissona Xili HQ
Location
Guangdong
Completion 2008

c Coco-Mat Store
Location
Shenzen
Completion 2009

Hallucinate Design Office is a multidisciplinary award-winning design organization working creatively in the fields of interior, graphic and architecture. It was founded in 2007 by Wenliang Wang, born in 1967. The studio holds on to professional attitude, interpreting and exploring the relation between space and humankind, and aims to create new design paradigms. The architects of the office coming from different expertise and cultural backgrounds, work on a wide range of project scope from high-end commercial projects to the most creative and fun works. For Hallucinate the core values of design are thoughts and reflection based on its constant consideration towards people, things, happenings, and surroundings. The studio endows its works with its own unique design language and philosophy.

a

b

c

Midwest Inland Port Financial Town

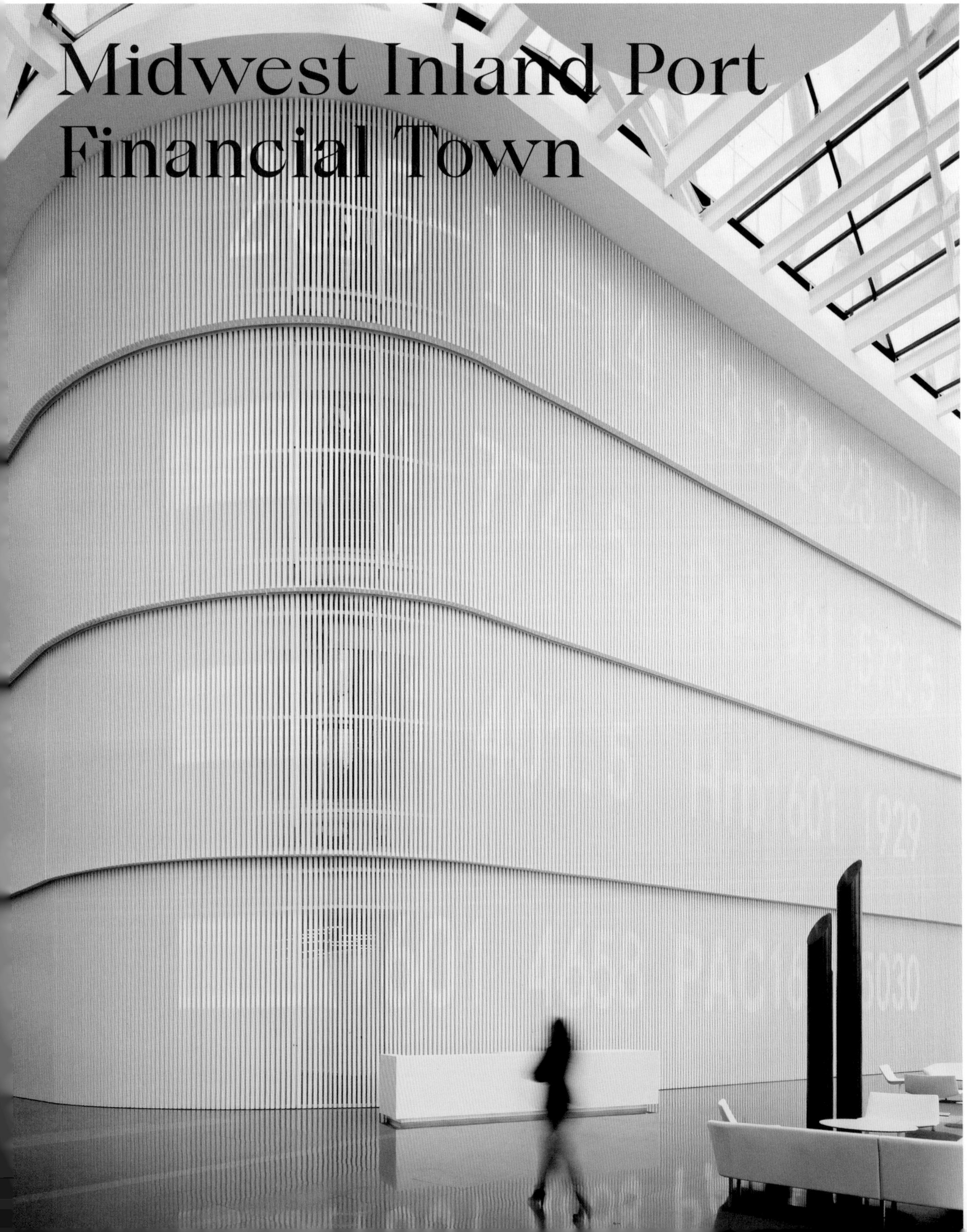

Location
99 Gangwu Boulevard, Xi'an International Logistics Park, Xi'an, China

Building type commercial

Completion 2016

Client Maike Group

Gross floor area 320,000 m^2

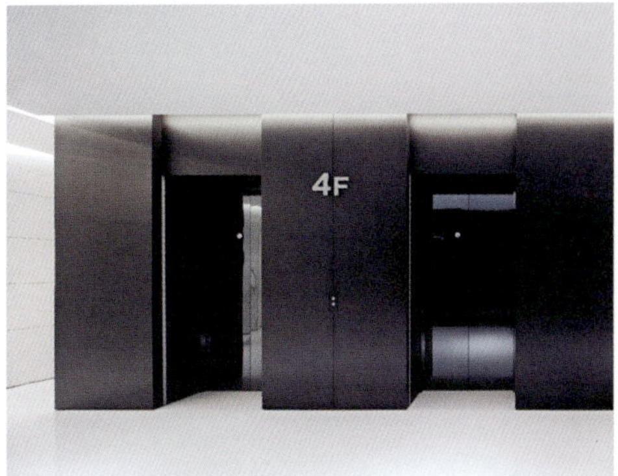

a

b

Financial Town is a modern trading and logistics platform that offers integrated transportation, warehousing, freight forwarding and information services. The project was created for Maike Metals Group which is one of the biggest non-ferrous metal suppliers and traders. The interior design of Financial Town was designed beyond the city's geographical features for a balanced presentation of historical elements in an open perspective. An open and tranquil style was used and the design features a luminous roof and the large-gridded digital walls that blur the boundaries between reality and imagination. Modern technology and the architecture itself create a surreal surrounding. Light falls in through the three black metal pillars of different heights to the ceiling of the lobby and forms a diffuse reflection through the geodesic dome. The interior walls are covered with grids formed by tailor-made extruded aluminum sections of special dimensions melded with LED P60 electronic display units. Hallucinate has intentionally abandoned the conventional approach in pursuing softer boundaries between the three dimensions in order to enable a smooth, undisrupted visual sight from the floor all up to the ceiling. In the lecture hall, the ceiling comes in the shape of folded paper to reduce sound reflections and avoid excessive light onto the presentation screen. Overall Financial Town is a fascinating place of modern and futuristic vision which combines design and technology.

a Elevator hall
b Atrium
c Meeting room
d Lecture hall
e Lobby with modern lighting
f Lobby with modern furniture
g Ground floor plan
h Site plan

c

d

e f

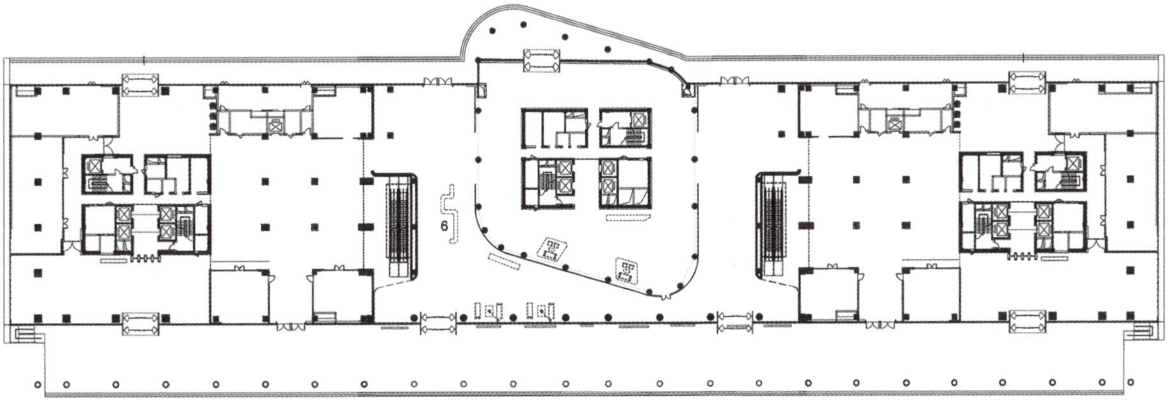

g

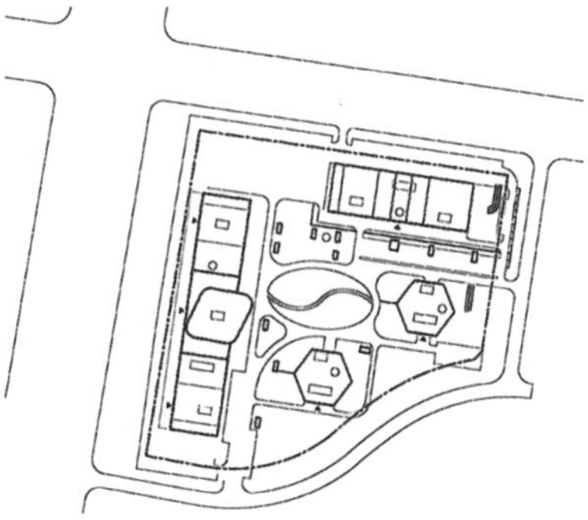

h

Interval Architects

Yunduan Gu, Oscar Ko

a **Raffles Kindergarten Complex**
Location
Huailai
Completion 2017

b **House G**
Location
Shanghai
Completion 2019

c **1 Half Stadium**
Location
Beijing
Completion 2013

Interval Architects is a Shanghai-based architectural design practice co-founded in 2012 by Oscar Ko, born in 1981, and Yunduan Gu, born in 1984. It critically examines issues relating to urbanism, architecture and the environment. The studio believes that architecture should possess qualities that reflect specifities of its context and become a spatial production that belongs to a certain place and time. Interval Architects has won many awards as for example the Silver Prize in World Architecture News Awards in the category Emerging Practice of the Year and Architecture MasterPrize Small Firm of the Year. It also has been longlisted in Dezeen Awards - Emerging Architect of the Year category. Its works have also been widely presented in exhibitions such as Beijing Urban and Architecture Biennale 2020 Pilot Exhibition.

a

b

c

Location
Hengshui Botanic Park,
Hengshui 053000,
Hebei, China
Building type culture
Completion 2018
Client Hengshui
Botanic Park
Gross floor area 2,065 m²

Tower of Bricks

a

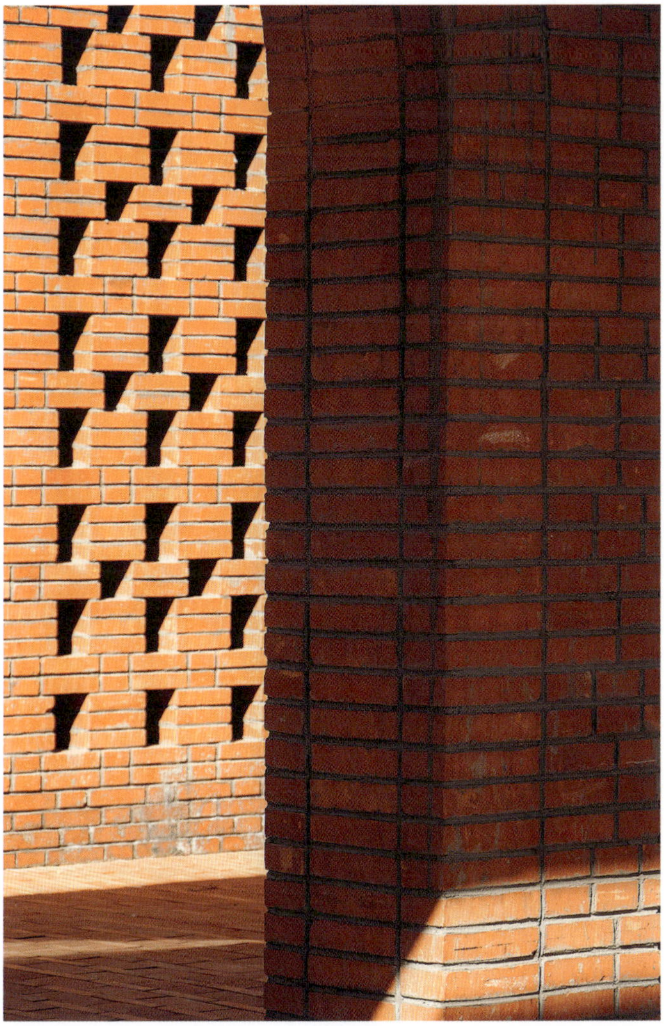

b

The project began with an abandoned Hoffman brick kiln located on the site where Interval Architects was asked to design a botanic art center in Hengshui Botanic Park. With the intention to respond to the specific history of the place and to recall the memory of the existence of the brick kiln, the new architecture has a spatial composition that references to the Hoffman brick kiln but equipped with contemporary functions and notions such as the idea of publicness, connectivity to the environment and user experience. The building was mainly created out of shale bricks and contains arches which make the inside appear light-flooded and welcoming. It functions as a gallery where art and ceramics can be experienced and admired by visitors. The main tower in the middle of the construction offers an impressive view on the swamp area. The whole project aims to create a direct connection between the past of the original brick factory and the present of the new exhibition space which is also made out of bricks in order to continue the original purpose of the place within the design.

a East façade
b Detail of brick façade
c East façade by the lake
d Side view elevation west
e Inner courtyard with the tower
f Detailed view outer façade
g Courtyard by the restaurant
h Detail of the wall section

c

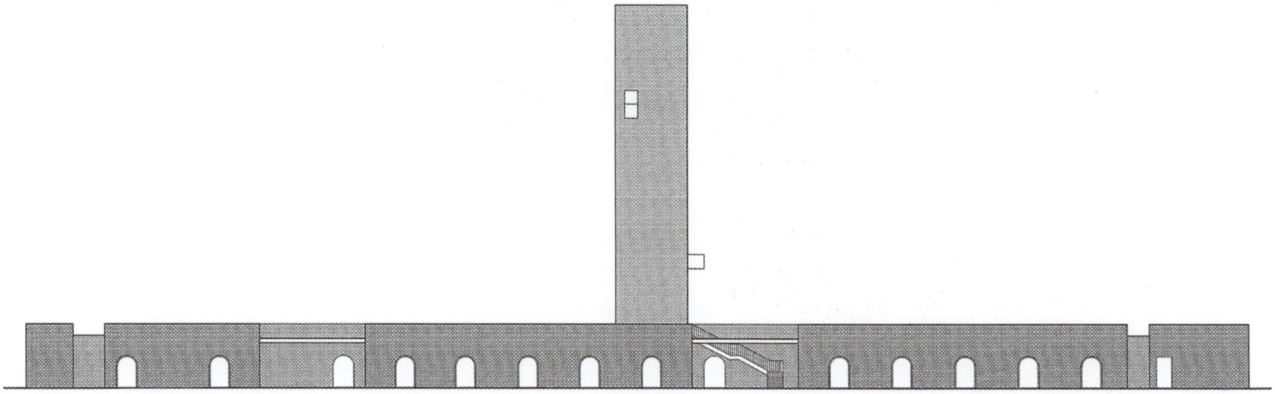

d

e f

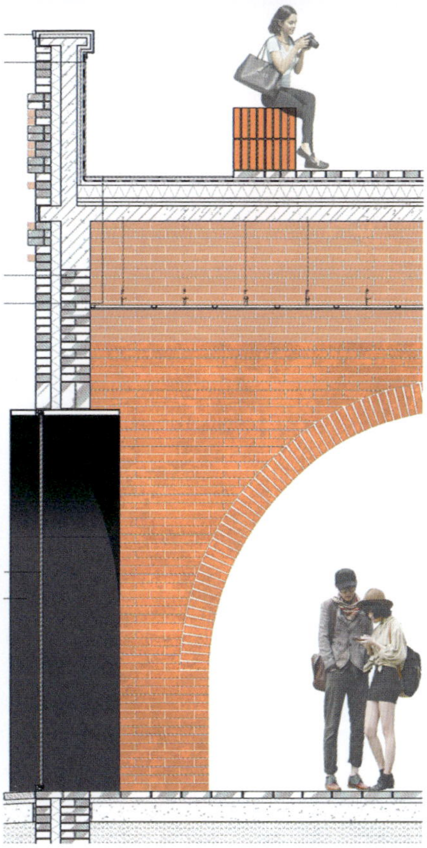

g h

Temp

Howard Jiho Kim

a **Cafe Parallel**
Location
Dongcheng, Beijing
Completion 2018

b **Amoon Optical**
Location
Xicheng, Beijing
Completion 2020

c **X Museum**
Location
Chaoyang, Beijing
Completion 2020

Howard Jiho Kim, born in 1984, founded the architectural design studio Temp in Beijing in 2017. He studied architecture at the University of Virginia, USA, worked before as a project architect at MAD Architects and led a studio at Tsinghua University Architectural Design Institute. Temp studio considers architecture as an exploration and at the same time expression of reality. In time of increasing conflicts of ambition, function, and place, Temp understands it as critical to extract relationships of simple organizations through clear logic and process. Therefore the studio constantly seeks forms of simplicity hidden behind the unpredictable world of different scales as for example objects, architecture, and city.

a

b

c

Ajia Teahouse

Location
15-4 Xixi Paradise, Xihu District, Hangzhou 310023, Zhejiang, China
Building type hospitality
Completion 2019
Client Beijing Ajia Culture Ltd.
Gross floor area 740 m²

a

b

Temp has designed a tea house in Xixi Wetland located at the west part of Hangzhou. Xixi Wetland is a national park densely packed with ponds, lakes, and swamps with 1,800 years of cultural heritage. The larger indoor space of the building was formed by placing private rooms for drinking tea. These rooms are scattered around with stone paths connecting each other. While they are walled off by bricks to create a certain level of privacy, wooden louvers and gaps within the walls offer a sense of opening. Varying levels of transparencies from heavy and solid to light and open form spaces of many layers. The tea house is mainly built with simple materials as bricks, wood, stones, and bamboo. Bricks are layered vertically with certain parts left porous. Wooden louvers slide or swing to open and close the tea rooms. Several pieces of furniture and a pavilion are made from local bamboo structured in tenon joints. The outdoor courtyard is stepped into different heights of granite stairs and platforms. Pools of water and trees divide the larger space and create shade for the seating areas. The Ajia Teahouse creates a place for drinking traditional Chinese tea in a modern way using simple materials. The project is spatially exploring to bring outdoor landscape indoors and to form layers of varying privacy and openness.

a Wooden tea room façade
b Division of interior space by bricks
c Floor plan
d Steel shelves embedded in bricks
e Courtyard steps lead to tearoom
f Stone steps create platforms
g Indoor landscape with stone

c

d e

f g

ZZHK Architects

Zhang Ke

a **Jinan Wanda Cultural Sports Tourism City**
Location
Jinan
Completion 2016

b **Holiday Inn Express**
Location
Qiliping
Completion 2019

c **Lake and Moon Houses**
Location
Heilongtan
Completion 2020

d **Museum of Peaks Valley**
Location
Chengdu
Completion 2018

In 2014, Zhang Ke, born in 1972, established ZZHK Architects as a professional elite architects' team dedicating on high-quality, technical strength, characteristics, and aesthetics. ZZHK Architects has completed project types including exhibition centers, commercial complexes, hotels, high-end clubhouses, top-class villas, and boutique residences. Some designs of the team were reported by international media. ZZHK Architects is widely recognized by the market for its unique modeling ability of landmark buildings and innovative design ability of high-quality house type. The team is well-established in Chengdu, participating in competitions national-wide and even worldwide.

a

b

c

d

Ruyi Bridge

Location
Dayuan Park, Tianfu 2nd Street, Chengdu, Sichuan, China
Building type infrastructure
Completion 2018
Client CDHT Investment
Gross floor area 1,151 m^2

Ruyi Bridge was designed on the design concept called Sound of Panpipes as the façade design is inspired by the Chinese panpipes, a traditional Chinese musical instrument. The undulations and fluttering of the bridge body simulate the fresh and elegant flow of music rhythm, shaping a functional urban sculpture. Viewed from above, the bridge resembles a Ruyi embedded in the city. Ruyi is a Chinese traditional S-shaped ornamental object usually made of jade. It formerly symbolizes good luck. Since the completion of the project in 2018, it has received several awards from international media. Especially at night the construction delights with its colorful pink-reddish lighting. The bridge is not only a crossing tool for the locals over the busy roads of Chengdu but has also become a magnet for visitors. Responsible for construction was the Southwest Municipal Engineering Design & Research Institute of China.

a S-shape of the construction
b Approach of bridge at night
c Bird's-eye view
d Close-up of the bridge
e Master plan

a

b

c

d

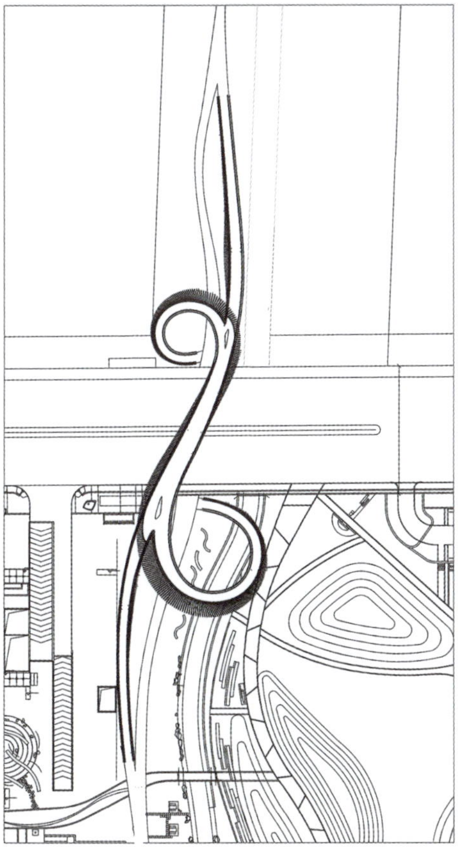

e

Yuan Ye Architects

Ye Yuan

a **Memory House**
Location
Beijing
Completion 2020

b **The Hill of Play**
Location
Beijing
Completion 2019

c **Tangshan Library**
Location
Hebei
Completion 2016

d **Reconstruction of Jiang Village**
Location
Henan
Completion 2019

Yuan Ye Architects is a research-oriented architecture studio rooted in China with international vision and influence. It was founded in 2010 by Ye Yuan, born in 1975. The studio combines academic, creative and engineering closely, carries out all-round design practice in the fields of architecture, urban space and landscape, and seeks innovative solutions to solve the contemporary problems in China. The studio constantly explores the boundary of architecture and the possible prospect of urban future, in order to respond to the history, culture and spirit of the times. It has been rewarded with many awards as the Gold award of China Architectural Design Awards or the Architectural Achievement Award of WAACA Awards. Yuan Ye Architects follows three main principals: simple and unadorned design, meaningful form and architecture for ordinary and all kinds of people.

a

b

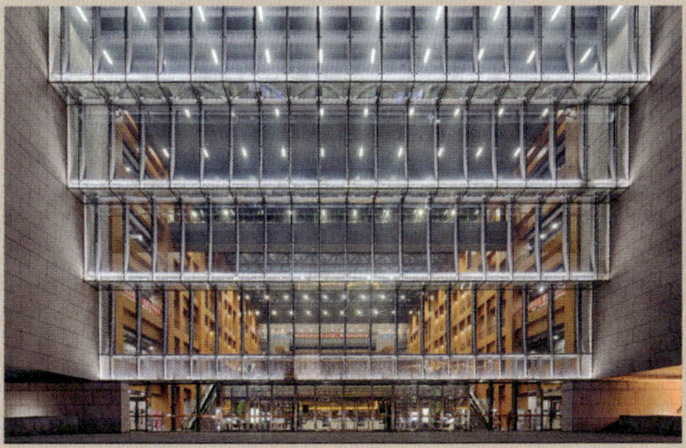
c

d

Bozhou Gymnasium

Location
Mudan Road, Qiaocheng District, Bozhou, Anhui, China
Building type sports facility
Completion 2018
Client CJHG
Gross floor area 48,650 m²

a

b

The Bozhou Gymnasium can accommodate more than 6,000 spectators. It includes a sports competition hall, a training hall and a relatively independent national fitness center, which takes into account the different social needs of the game time and non competition time, and creates conditions for the sustainable operation in the later period. For the construction the architects abstracted the inverted trapezoid from the buildings and artifacts of the Han Dynasty as the basic geometric form of the building, and used the square pool along the shape as the base to foil the building form. The architectural skin was inspired by the local armor of the warriors of the Han Dynasty with perforated aluminum plates and a continuous triangular folding surface. This surface of the epidermis also opens like a curtain, which naturally opens in the middle and forms the entrance of the building. A circle of half indoor and half outdoor public hall was designed between the main function volume and the outdoor environment as a buffering space for people to gather, distribute and communicate. The steel grid structure of the roof, the three-dimensional truss on the side and the hollow metal skin form a rich light and shadow effect under the sunlight. The building also contains sustainable aspects such as a rainwater recovery and recycling system, natural ventilation and lighting systems and a solar photovoltaic and hot water system. The project was created in cooperation with China Construction Design Group as design agency.

a Entrance perspective
b Shared hall
c Interior of gymnasium
d Entrance
e Gymnasium perspective
f Aerial view
g Steel construction
h Construction sketch

c

d e

f

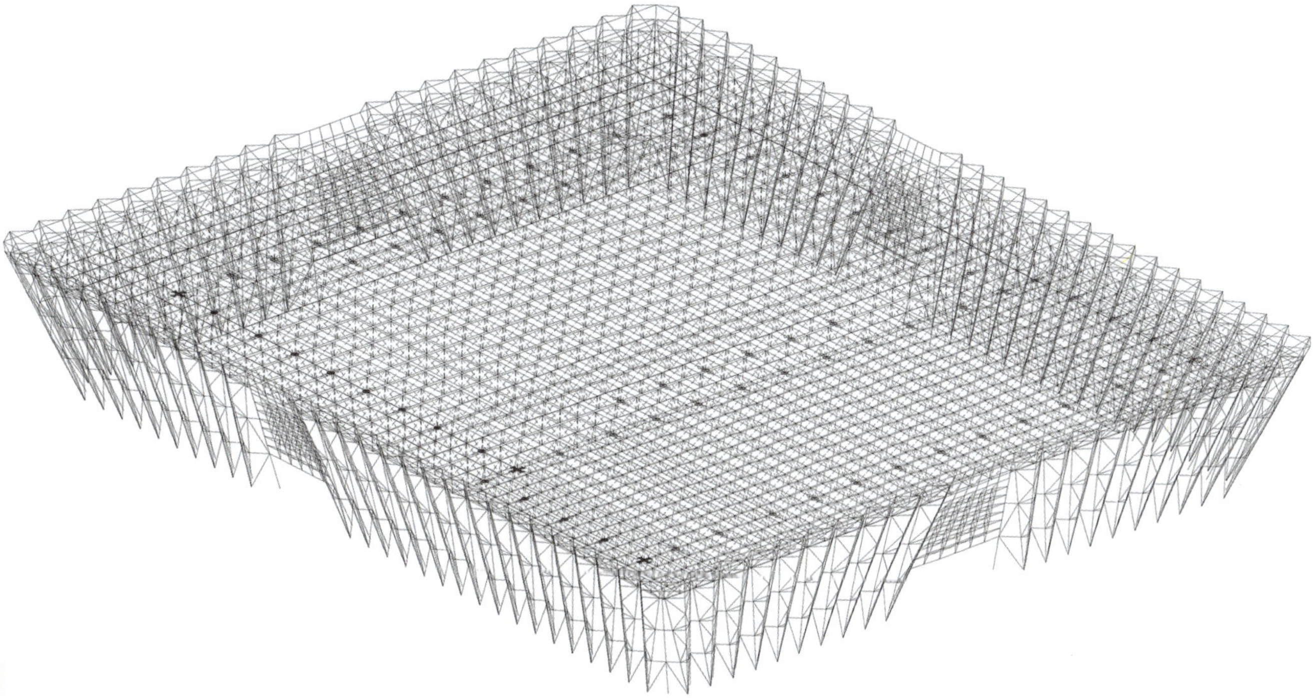

g

h

Atelier XÜK

Xu Zhang, Kenan Liu

a **Qinglongshan Park Multifunction Hall**
Location
Yixing
Completion 2019

b **Sury No.3 Hotel**
Location
Huzhou
Completion 2017

c **Container Showroom**
Location
Shanghai
Completion 2014

Kenan Liu, born in 1979, and Xu Zhang, born in 1978, established Atelier XÜK in 2010 in Shanghai. Both of them have been conducting design studios respectively at Tongji University in Shanghai and Southeast University in Nanjing. The practice of Atelier XÜK focuses on recording the ephemeral moments of the rapid transformation process in both urban and rural areas of China. It has completed projects of various types and scales in different regions across China. In 2020, Atelier XÜK was awarded the Youth Exploration Award of the Architecture China Award. This award was initiated by the Pritzker Prize Laureate Wang Shu. With a jury consisting of world-renowned architects and scholars such as Yung Ho Chang, Benedetta Tagliabue, Iwan Baan, and Philip Ursprung, it is the most influential award in East Asia.

a

b

c

Lostvilla Qinyong Primary School Hotel

Location
Qinyong Village,
Ningbo, China
Building type mixed-use
Completion 2018
Client lostvilla
Gross floor area 2,000 m²

a

b

In the 1970s, the original village houses of Qinyong Village were completely demolished and reconstructed. The fabric of the natural village was replaced with a neatly organized uniform grid. The whole village was built with local brown granite. The uniform row houses under the commune system show a completely different idea of landscape structure from the traditional villages in the patriarchal society. The village renovation includes public buildings such as a primary school, a canteen, a guest house, a hotel and an auditorium, all made of wood and steel. The primary school is located on the high platform at the northernmost end of the village and consists of a main teaching building and an auxiliary building. The elevated platform that runs through the rooms and corridors was a key design method and the interior elements can be comprehensively arranged on the platform. The orientation and topological relationship of the rooms differs on different floors, responding to the specific concerns of function and window position. A canteen was added on the rooftop of the annex building. The added part adopts a light steel structure which is welded by five times five centimeter big square steel rods. A staircase on the northern side of the annex building opens in several directions. Fabricated woodwork from furniture scale to room scale was used in order to create an unique experience for visitors who are supposed to be inspired to escape the flow of commonness.

a Aerial view on village and school
b View from the village
c Ground floor plan
d View from the canteen on village
e Inner design with woodwork
f Façade of the main building
g Added canteen with staircases
h Section of annex building

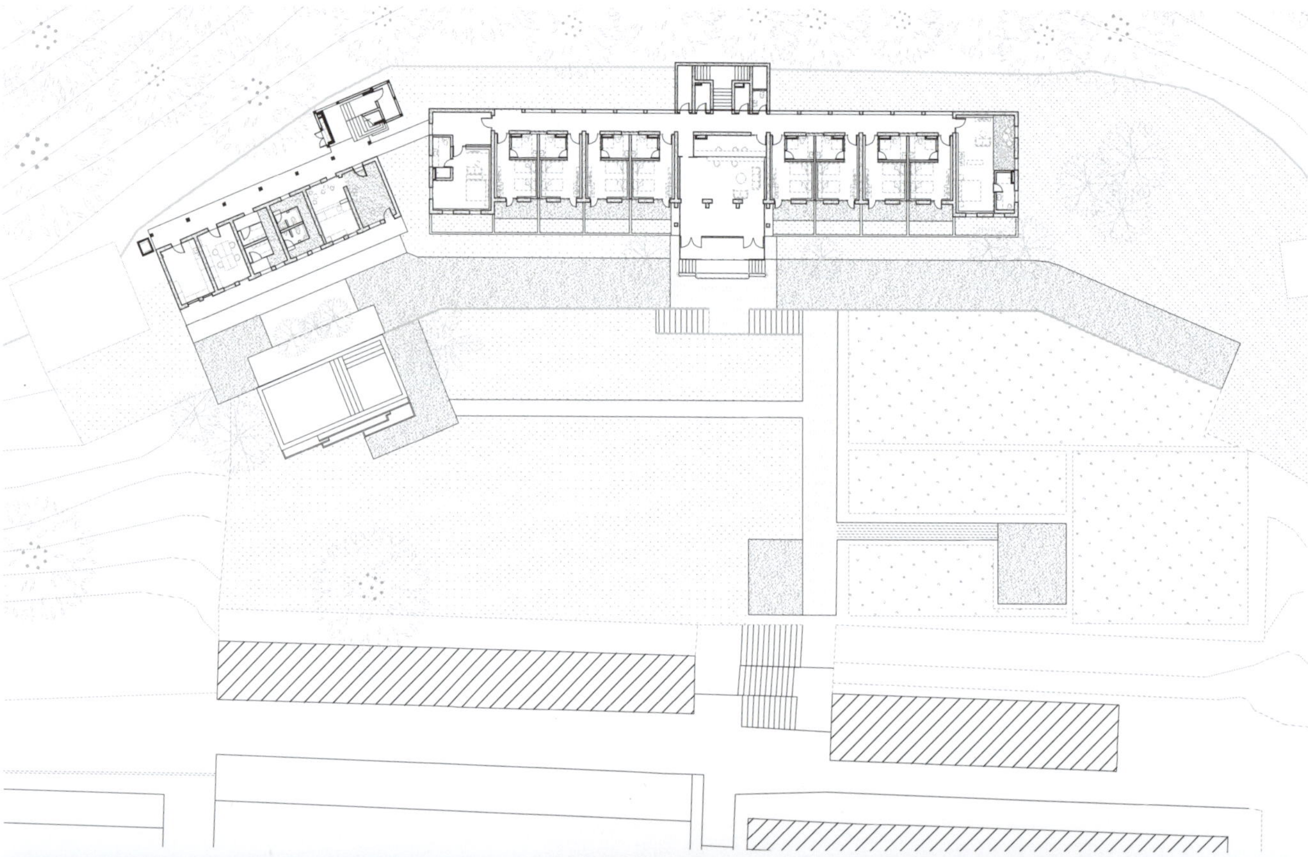

c

d

e

f g

h

SWA Group

René Bihan

Ye Luo

Jim Lee

a **PayPal Headquarters**
Location
San José, CA, USA
Completion 2017

b **Chase Center**
Location
San Francisco, CA, USA
Completion 2019

c **Poly Pazhou Inernational Plaza**
Location
Guangzhou
Completion 2016

d **University of Monterrey**
Location
Monterrey, Mexico
Completion 2017

SWA is an international landscape architecture, planning, and urban design firm known for the creativity, responsiveness, and resilience of its work. Across the firm's nine studios, more than 200 professionals work worldwide on projects ranging from city districts, campus design, and commercial complexes to boutique resorts and charming urban plazas. The San Francisco studio is led by the principals Jim Lee, born in 1953, René Bihan, born in 1960, and Ye Luo, born in 1976. SWA projects are diverse in both form and location. The firm was founded in 1957 and has contributed to more than 800 award-winning projects in 60 countries. SWA partners with clients to create vibrant places that are at once ecologically resilient, aesthetically compelling, and socially beneficial.

a

b

c

d

Location
Beijing, China
Building type mixed-use
Completion 2017
Client Poly Real Estate Group
Gross floor area 10,000 m²

Poly Future City

a

b

Poly Future Metropolitan (phase one) is centrally located in the core of Changping Future Science City, north of downtown Beijing. Created by SWA San Francisco, which was also responsible for the landscape architecture, and BIAD as building architect, the project supports the government's expectations for technological innovation and future urban growth in the capital city. The Welcome Center pursues an agile, light-filled elegance. While the small single building's site lacks presence in the larger urban context, SWA San Fransisco's design gives it legibility from the street. The landscape design is futuristic in nature, yet simple and elegant in materials and human in function. Along the main frontage road, a series of mirrored stainless-steel walls and folded landforms create sculpted plinth edges. Water planes are extended along the base of the building. Two large stone wedge fountains frame the main entries to the upper plaza. An elegant water veil transfers water from the plinth level to the sidewalk level. Water falls through a serrated stone weir, which gives an elegant glittering edge along the plinth while the other side is a ragged edge. The plaza is filled with lights along with paving stripes, and seems to extend beyond the site's boundaries. The design blends interior and exterior space. It is supposed to create a place for relaxation away from the bustle of city life.

a Water veil invites in plaza area
b Water planes at the base
c Entire construction plan
d Seating area outside
e Outer design sketch
f Front view with artistic designs
g Garden facing the indoor
h Detail of water play
i Slotted waterfall

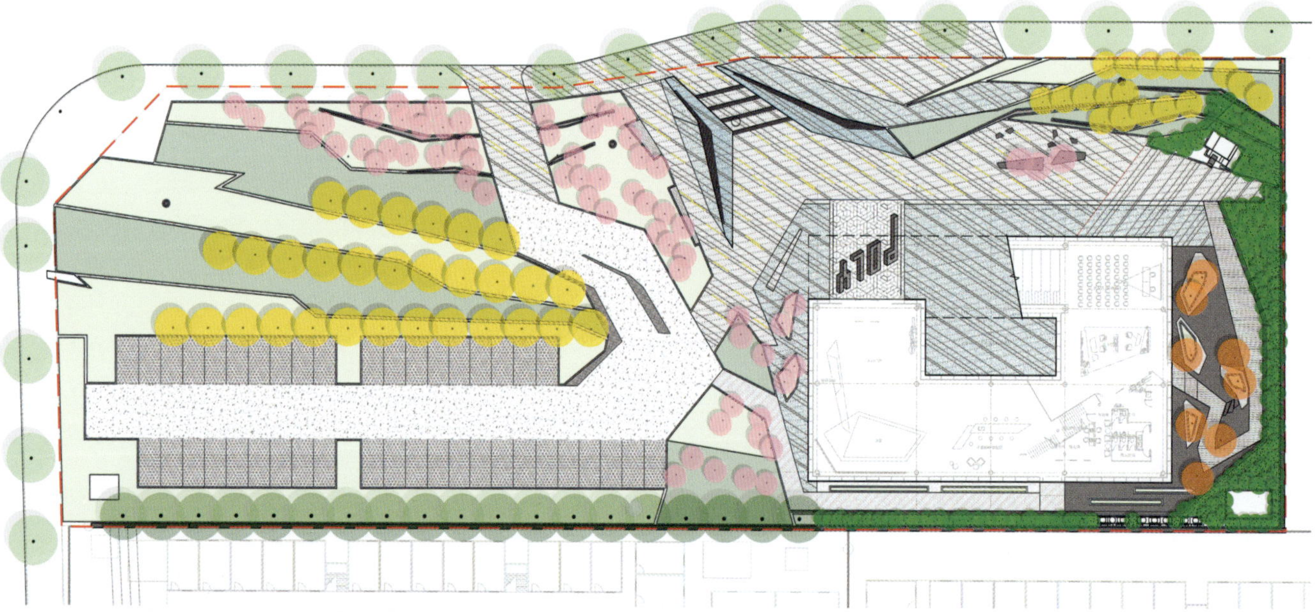

c

d

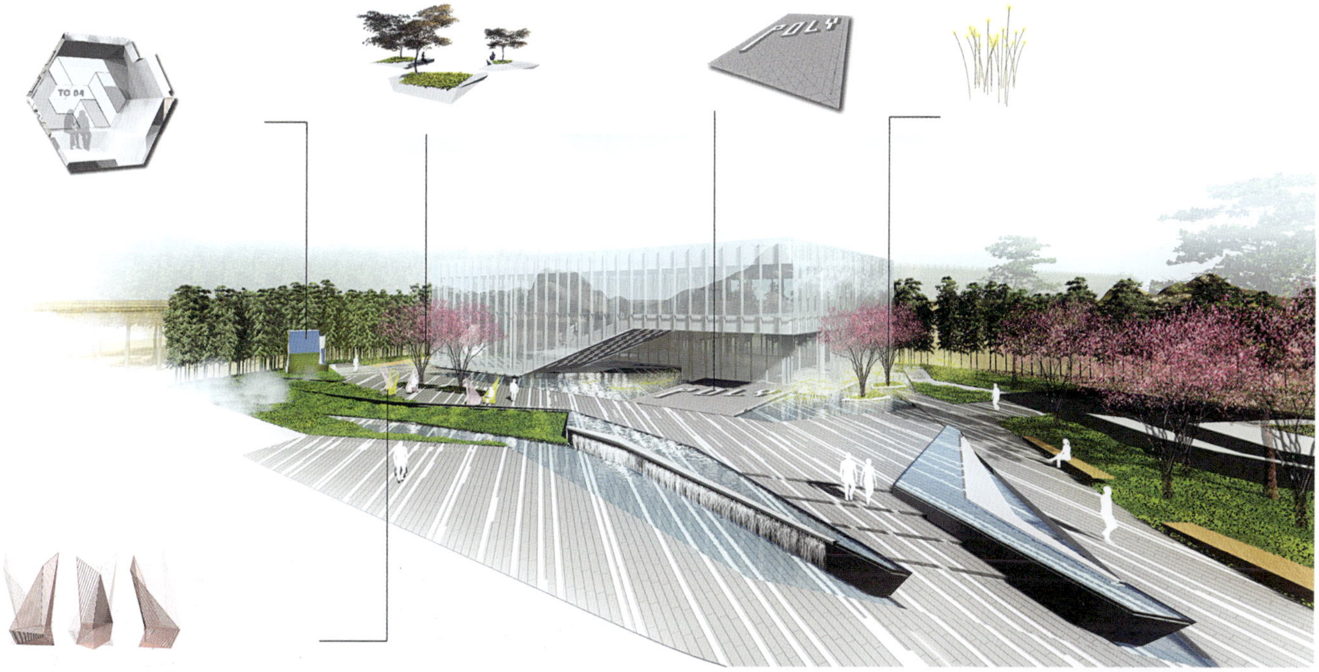

e

f g

h i

Neri&Hu Design and Research Office

Lyndon Neri

Rossana Hu

a **The Brick Wall | Tsingpu Yangzhou Retreat**
Location
Yangzhou
Completion 2017

b **The Sanctuary | Suzhou Chapel**
Location
Suzhou
Completion 2016

c **The Lantern | Sulwhasoo Flagship**
Location
Seoul, South Korea
Completion 2016

d **The Void | Aranya Art Center**
Location
Qinhuangdao
Completion 2019

e **Sculpted Light | New Shanghai Theater**
Location
Shanghai
Completion 2016

Neri&Hu Design and Research Office was founded in 2006 by Lyndon Neri, born in 1965, and Rossana Hu, born in 1968. The practice's global portfolio includes commissions ranging from master planning and architecture, to interior design, installation, furniture, product, branding and graphic works. The studio is composed of multicultural staff speaking over 30 different languages. It has expanded the conventional boundaries of practice to include complementary disciplines and sees critical probing into the specificities of program, site, function, and history as essential to the creation of rigorous work. The office has been recognized by a number of prestigious international awards spanning the fields of architecture, interior, product and graphic design including most recently the Madrid Design Festival Award and the Design for Asia Grand Award 2020.

a

b

c

d

e

Number 31

Location
322 Jiaozhou Road, Building 31, Jing'an District, Shanghai, China
Building type office
Completion 2020
Client Neri&Hu Design and Research Office
Gross floor area 2,400 m²

The site for renovation of this project was a four-story nondescript office and dormitory building which was transformed by embracing its already existing potential. The ambition was to build upon the notion of a design commune. Apart from the inclusion of their own office in the building on the third and fourth floor and Design Republic offices on the second, it also contains an art gallery, a bakery and furniture store. A staircase stitches together the main building with a few communal spaces like co-working and open kitchen facilities on the second floor, a multipurpose event space as well as a rooftop garden. The first renovation strategy was a reworking of the main façade, to completely shift its proportions and reading, without any major structural alterations. The repetitive and perfunctory windows of the existing building got partially in-filled with glass bricks, while the bottom portion of new operable windows was strung together with a unifying black metal frame, creating the illusion of long horizontal ribbon windows. The entire upper part of the building received a coating of dark gray paint, while the ground floor showcases a different material treatment with glazed green tiles and a deep canopy being added atop. Different aspects of design were deployed reaching from architecture and interiors to furniture.

a Building façade
b Workplace
c Staircase connecting levels
d Seating and meeting area
e Construction plan
f Section

a

b c

d

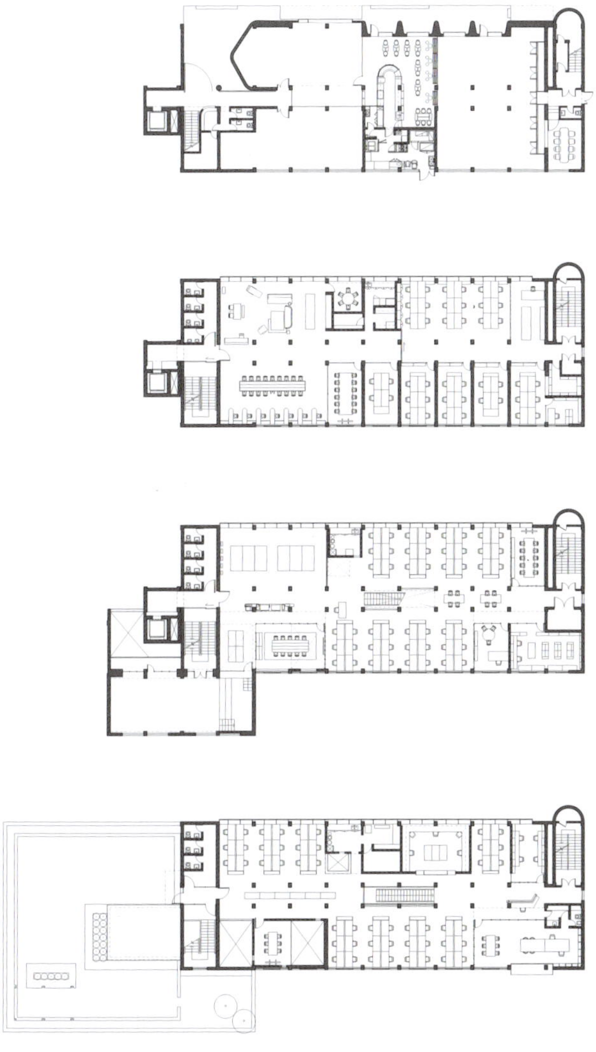

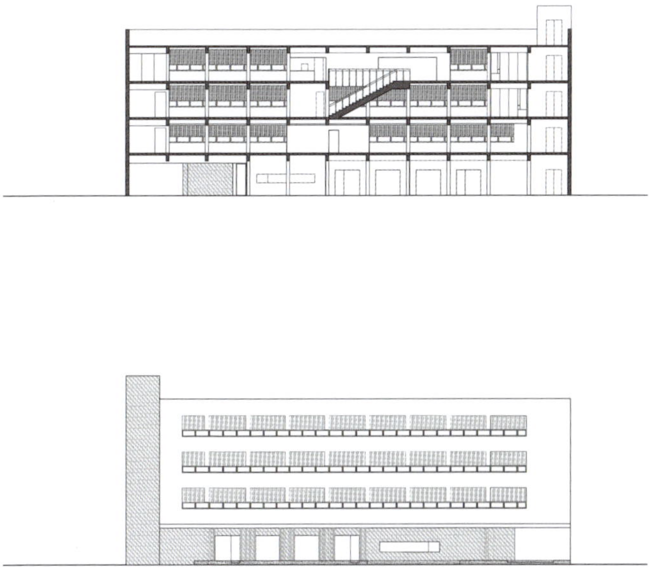

e f

O&O Studio

Suzanne Li

Eric Chan

Katt Chung Yap

a **Atelier Intimo Changzhou**
Location
Changzhou
Completion 2020

b **Mooncraft**
Location
Shanghai
Completion 2019

c **Atelier Intimo Ningbo**
Location
Ningbo
Completion 2020

The Hong Kong-based O&O Studio has an "Out and Outer" aspiration providing architecture, interior, art installation, and furniture design services. The award-winning design studio was co-founded in 2018 by Suzanne Li and Eric Chan, born in 1981 and 1979 respectively, with Katt Chung Yap, born in 1979, joining later in 2019. O&O believes that each design shall originate from a critical and cohesive process of strategic and visual thinking through to the end users' evaluation. This leads to the foundation for the next even more successful project. The studio does not serve standardized formula, but is recognized for nurturing influential design morphology that delivers fresh values to each commission. O&O has been awarded with the A' Design Award, the Fourth China New Power Interior Design Award and the China Interior Design 40under40 Award.

a

b

c

Atelier Intimo Flagship

Location
Unit 841, Renmin Fang, Huai Hai Lu, Shanghai, China

Building type commercial

Completion 2020

Client Atelier Intimo

Gross floor area 180 m²

a

b

The world has been hit by an unprecedented virus and natural disasters in 2020. Atelier Intimo's first flagship store designed by O&O Studio is inspired by the concept of "Rebirth of the Scorched Earth": It implies the integration of nature's healing power that gives mankind new hope. O&O wants to craft a dramatic space that allows visitors to spend moments imagining and fantasizing in such time and space. The flagship store is not an ordinary retail space, it is a performing stage for the lingerie brand. 3D printing, diatom mud paint, as well as custom-made stainless steel and carpet, have been used to give the two-story development its unique look, with the theatrical lighting design collaborated between O&O and Re-Sense. A series of art installations is also evolved through harmonizing the routine mannequins with the same design concept to fully demonstrate the brand's true characteristics. Designed by O&O as well with a slightly peculiar manner, these quirky archetypes act as the performing team on stage while allowing the visitors' endless imagination and interpretation on their portrayals.

a Ground floor retail space
b View to entrance
c Ground floor retail space
d Art installation series
e Mannequin display
f Art installation series
g Ground and first floor plan
h Section perspective east
i Section perspective west

c

d

e f

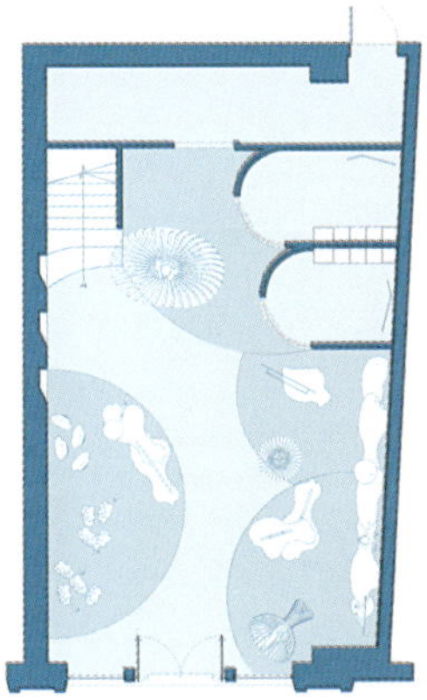
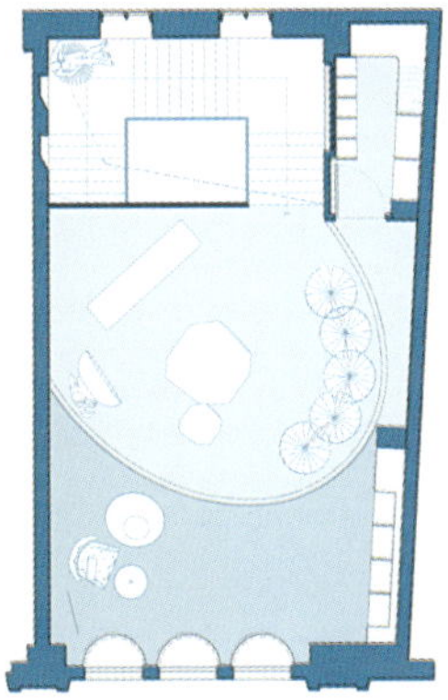
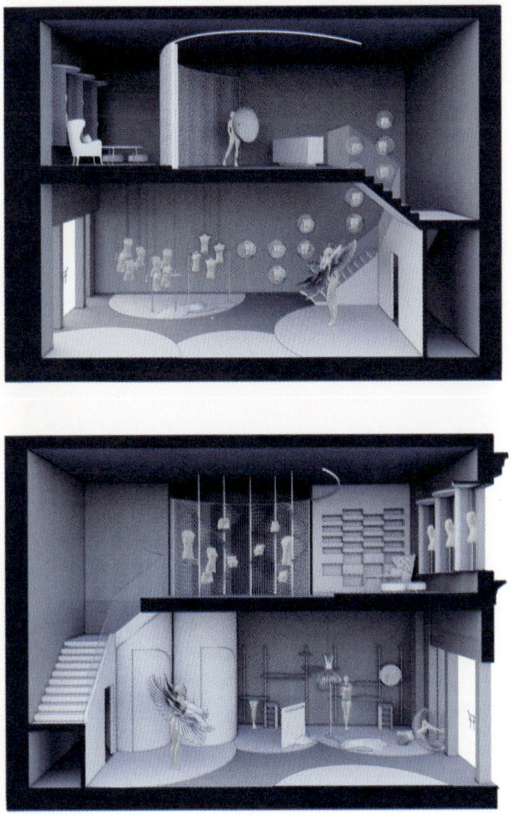

g h

i

aoe

Larry Wen

a Sunac One Central Mansion Sales Pavilion
Location
Chongqing
Completion 2018

b One Sino Park
Location
Chongqing
Completion 2020

c Shanxiao Sales Pavilion
Location
Chongqing
Completion 2019

d ShuiFa Info Town Property Exhibition Center
Location
Jinan
Completion 2020

Architect Larry Wen, born in 1968, founded the architecture and interior design studio aoe in Beijing in 2016. Its award-winning work spans residential, commercial, hospitality, educational, civic, corporate, mixed-use and urban planning markets. Underpinned by a creative intelligence-led philosophy, aoe intervenes in the social environment to create vibrant human-city spaces of the future. Responsive to modern facets of human life, aoe's design solutions fuse science and technology with the arts and culture, resulting in an inspired and much-needed reinvention of urban living – while constantly respecting local cultures, nature, and different ways of life. Larry studied at Cal Poly Pomona University and has since led several renowned global design companies, among them Aedas, Woods Bagot and Aecom, directing numerous well-known projects.

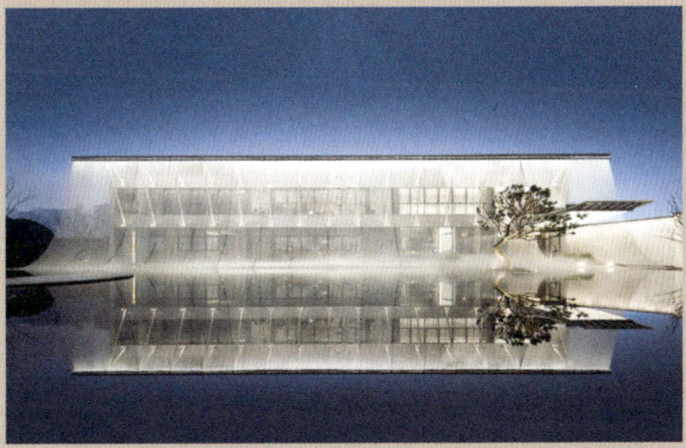
a

b

c

d

Courtyard NO.1

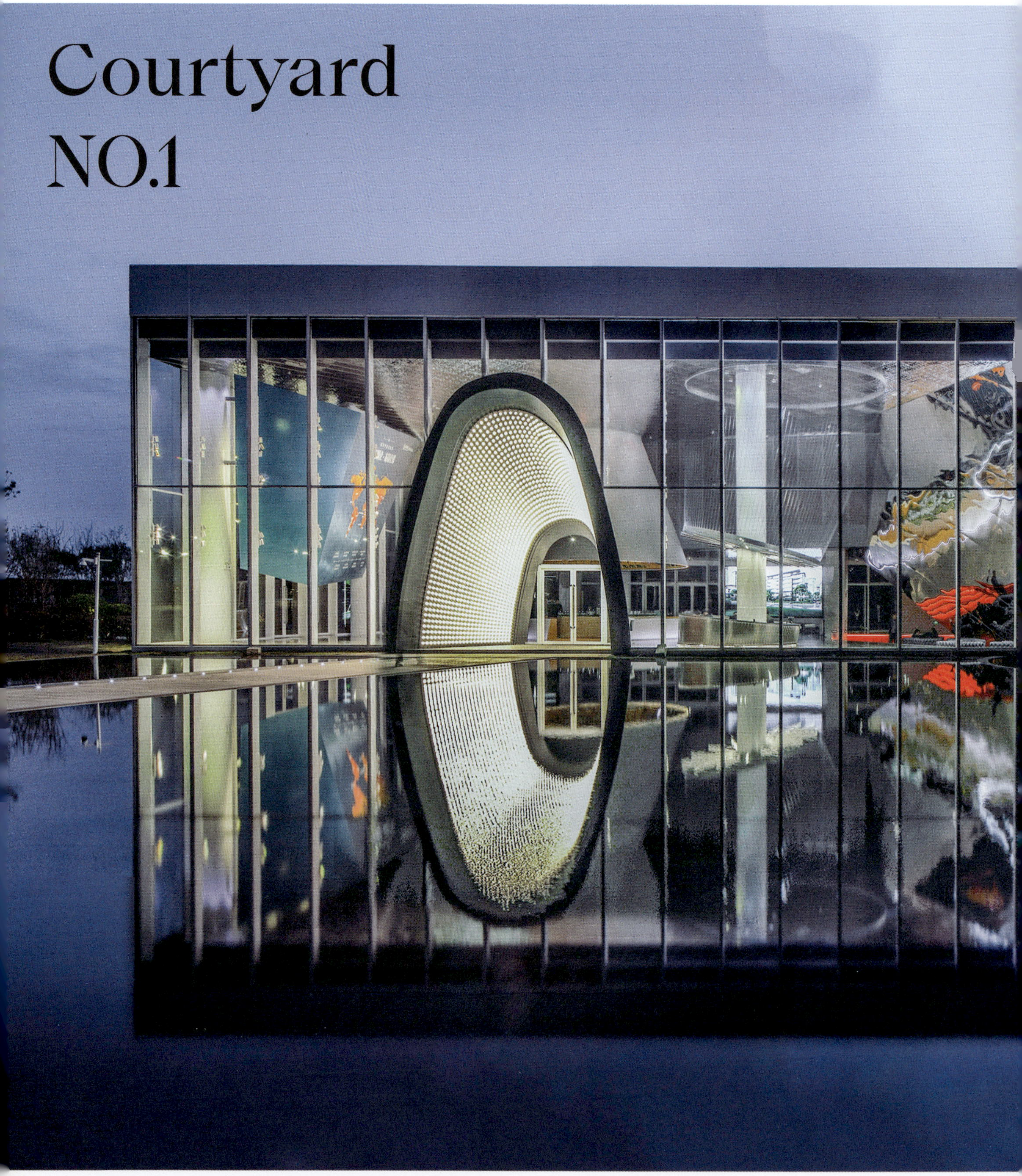

Location
Guangzhou Road, Economic Development Zone, Heze, Shandong, China
Building type commercial
Completion 2019
Client Shaanxi Construction Engineering Group Corporation Limited
Gross floor area 1,560 m^2

As China's development and urbanization continues, sales offices have become an important conduit for property developers to demonstrate their brand. These offices are not only community activity centers and lounge areas, but also a promotional window to attract more clients to buy properties. After most of the properties have been sold, however, the usefulness of these offices declines. The purpose of Courtyard NO.1 is to reconsider the special function of these buildings and make them more sustainable by becoming a symbolic public building for the future community and city. Courtyard NO.1 provides an impressive public space to local residents. As a reflection of the real world, this project attempts to look beyond a single function of the sales office through improved design, so that it can enhance the quality of public life, lead people to strive for a better future and make a positive contribution to the community. The architectural concept is based on the artistic suprematism that reflected the social and technological changes of the 1920s, with the intention of expressing the mutual influence and interdependence between physical and virtual space in the digital age. Therefore, the objects in the building are designed to float in an unstable state. The building façade is made of ultra-white glass which makes the interior visible to the outside space.

a Red gathering space
b Lighting cone above model area
c View through ultra-white glass
d Plan from above
e Outer façade
f Stainless steel metal panels

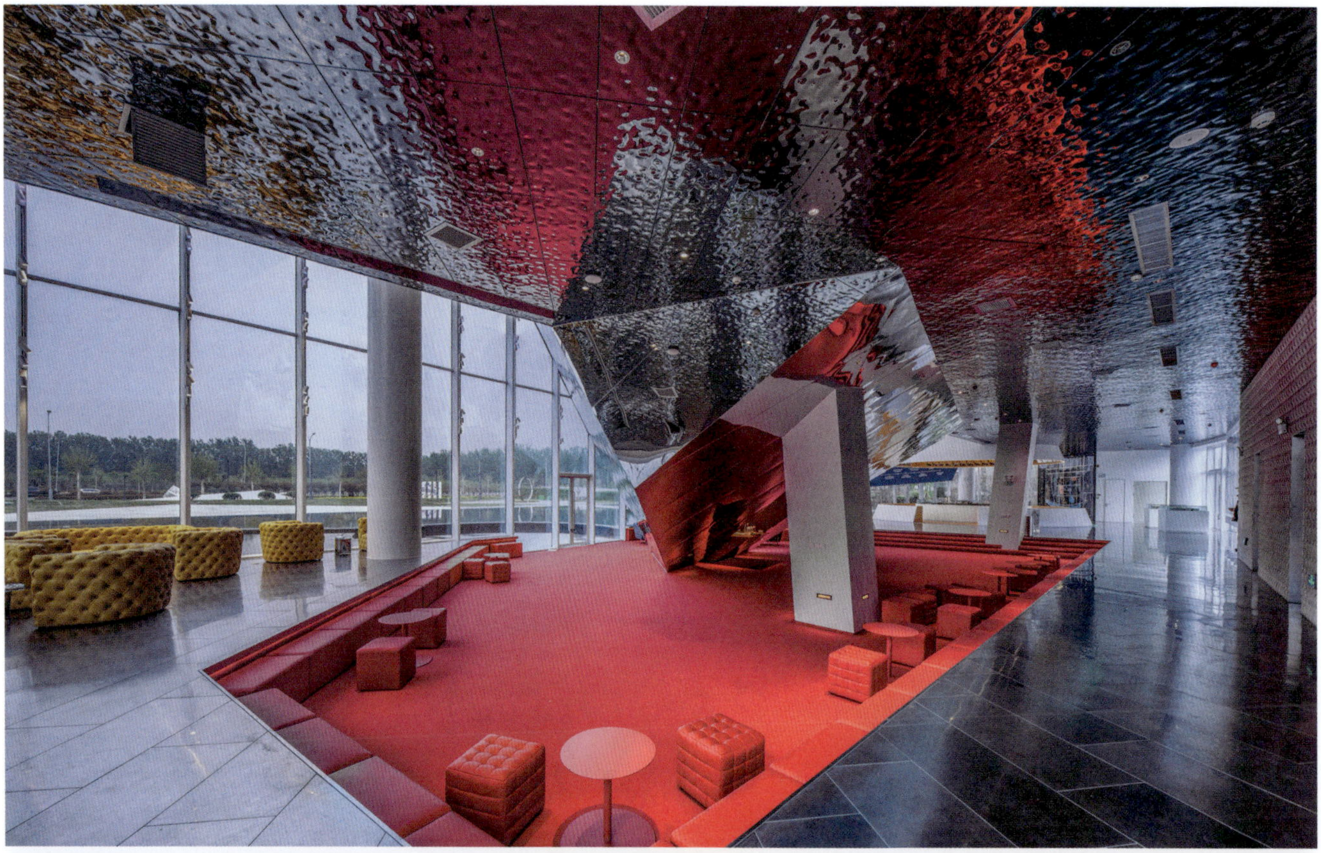

a

b

c

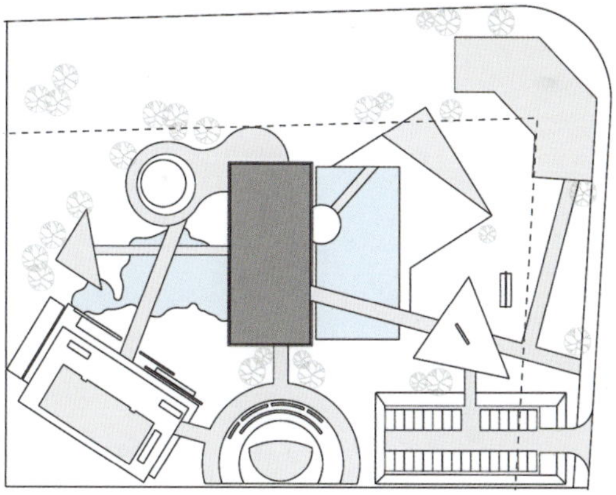

d

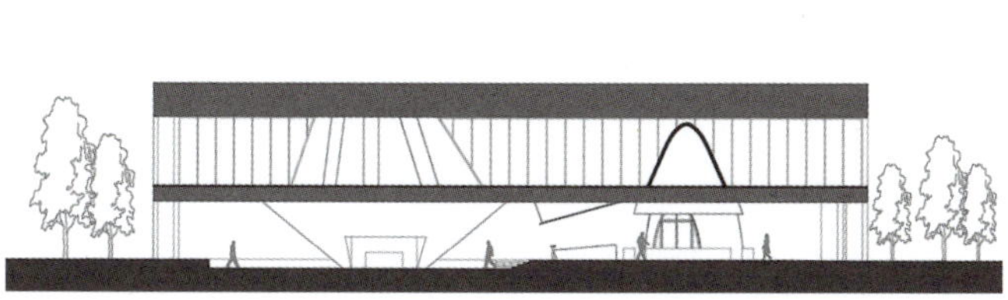

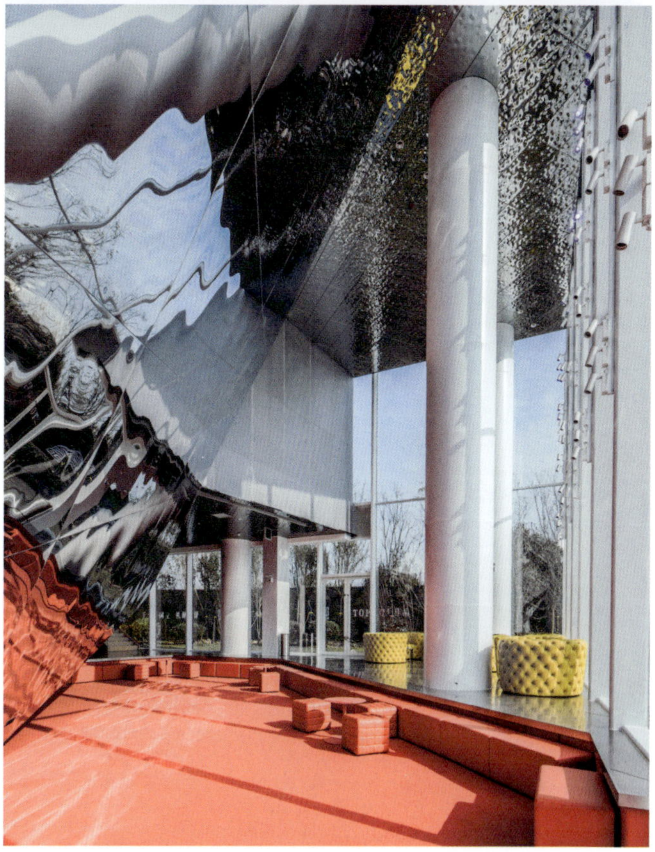

e f

Benjai Architecture

Qiao Xuesong

Li Xiang

a **Qinhuangdao**
Location
Hebei
Completion 2020

b **Zhumadian**
Location
Henan
Completion 2020

c **Yantai**
Location
Shandong
Completion 2020

d **Xi'an**
Location
Shanxi
Completion 2020

Benjai Architecture was founded in 2011 by Qiao Xuesong, born in 1976, and Li Xiang, born in 1983. The office is an enterprise engaged in architectural design since a long time. Designers from different countries who combine elements of nature, culture and era to conduct creative and practical exchanges belong to Benjai Architecture. What they pursue is that every project designed by Benjai is the joint efforts and creative idea of their clients and partners. These works of art will illustrate the harmonious humanity and comfortable life. The office has undertaken a number of important projects since 2011. It has a wide range of design interests, with a particular focus on commercial real estate, hotels, green buildings, luxury residential and other areas and upholds the integrity of people, the pursuit of perfection of the purpose of continuous innovation to complete more and better design.

a

b

c

d

Location
51 Hubeilu Street,
Nanjing 210009, China
Building type commercial
Completion 2018
Client Seazen Group
Gross floor area 68,204.3 m²

Nanjing Injoy Plaza

a

b

The project is located in the famous Hunan Road business circle in Nanjing. The architect was inspired by the formation process of the Rain Flower Pepples: The flowing water (commercial traffic) scours out the unique shaped Rain Flower Pepples (commercial space). This design concept runs through and is fully embodied in the plane layout and the spatial form inside and outside. Each consumers movement seems random, like water flowing together, but perfect commercial space brings them in harmony with the stream. Overall the plan follows the design concept, the architecture's integral line is hale and hearty and the corner is rounded and mellow. A complete display interface is formed in the southeast, and a terraced stage is formed in the northwest by retreating layer by layer. The two main business entrances recede substantially inward, creating a gray space that resembles an elaborate urban reception room. Dazing color has broken the original dull environment here at night, giving out a feeling of fresh and lively breath in this busy life, and greatly improving the quality of business circle.

a Street view
b Main entrance
c Bird's-eye view
d Main entrance
e Central courtyard
f First floor plan
g Site plan

c

d

e

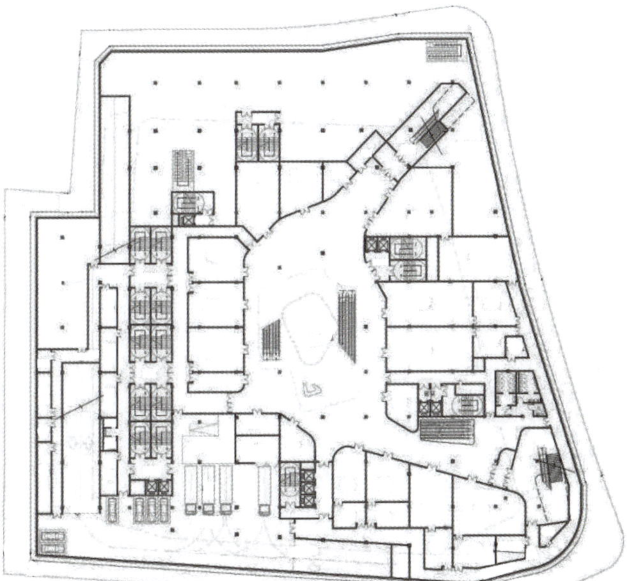

f g

RhineScheme

Lei Yang, Ran Li, Wolf Loebel

a Tianjin Culture Center
Location
Tianjin
Completion 2013

b IN-Beijing Soho
Location
Beijing
Completion 2012

c Xixi Park Visitors Center
Location
Hangzhou
Completion 2014

d Qingyifang Green Mall
Location
Changchun
Completion ongoing

RhineScheme Design Group was founded in 2004 and is managed by Wolf Loebel, born in 1962, Ran Li, born in 1974, and Lei Yang, born in 1980. Its Beijing studio serves as a joint home that connects all nine associated partners. The river Rhine as part of its name is a symbol of the free-flowing ideas that design processes have been feeding on from time immemorial. RhineScheme has realized countless worldwide projects spanning urban planning, architecture, interior architecture as well as landscape design. It has acquired an excellent reputation for extremely complex projects, especially in China. With nearly 160 employees in its branches in Beijing, Shanghai, Cologne, Hamburg, Leipzig, and Philadelphia, the practice can draw upon more than 35 years of experience in all relevant planning disciplines.

a

b

c

d

IPPH-Headquarters

Location
50 Qixiang Road, Haidian District, Beijing 100081, China

Building type office

Completion 2016

Client IPPH Beijing

Gross floor area 32,000 m²

a

b

Intellectual Property Publishing House, abbreviated by IPPH, deals with publishing of patent literature in books, magazines, and other media. The company's new headquarter is an up-to-date office building with a narrative architecture as part of a consistent urban concept. The plot, located in the north-western part of central Beijing, is defined by streets on two sides. By moving the building away from the streets, it receives wider east-west façades which is favorable to an office building. This also creates a public square at the street corner functioning as distinct name card to the owner-investor and its cultural matrix. The façade creates the vivid image of a bookshelf, with bigger and smaller, thinner and wider volumes. The first three floors and the first underground floor of the 60-meter tower are for retail and catering, while the remaining 12 levels provide office space. The project centers on the concept of cultural exchange, reflected in a building that distinguishes between public areas and places for work. Semi-public functions like a bar and restaurant, an exhibition area and a conference hall are placed in the top floor. Other meeting areas are close to several overlooking terraces.

a View from Qixiang Road
b North view with main entrance
c View on building and surrounding
d Office interior during construction
e Detail section outer façade
f Master plan
g Outer façade

c

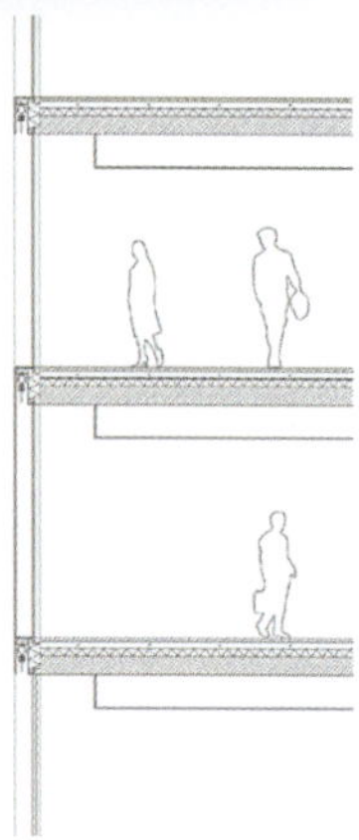

d e

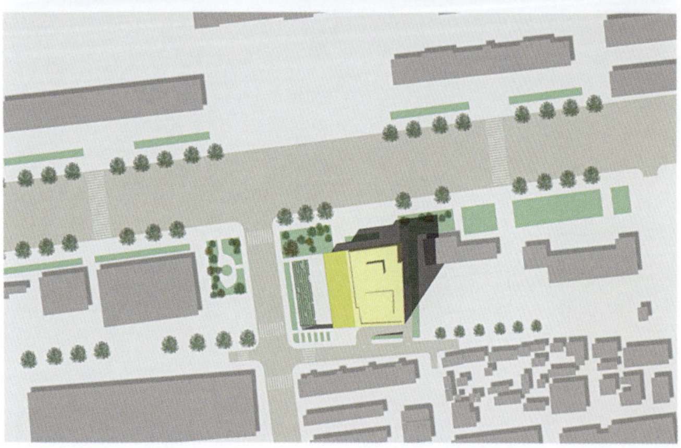

f

g

Continuation Studio

Jiujiang Fan

a **Courier Station**
Location
Jinhe Village
Completion ongoing

b **Building a "Mountain" in a Tiny Area**
Location
Hangzhou
Completion 2019

c **The Rotated House**
Location
Dinghai
Completion ongoing

Continuation Studio was founded in Hangzhou in 2015 by Jiujiang Fan, born in 1983. It is a research-based design studio with about 15 people working there. The studio insists on starting from basic architectural questions and aims at intelligent and poetic construction. It studies the content of all aspects of construction activities, concerns about landscape, material, structure, tectonics and form under a natural and cultural background. The team continues to intervene in community and urban construction in the way of space production. Continuation Studio believes that designers should have appropriate values and foresee-ability from the perspective of anthropology to utilize the relation among different architectures, users and designers, which continuously forms mutual influence and changes.

a

b

c

Location
Huangsha Village, Dinghai District, Zhoushan City, Zhejiang, China
Building type recreational
Completion 2020
Client Zhoushan Secret Land Guanhai Tourism Development Co., Ltd
Gross floor area 180 m²

The Terraced House

a

b

The Terraced House in Dinghai is a reception center in a decentralized home stay resort that functions as a coffee and breakfast restaurant and showroom. Situated above the road into the village, the exterior of The Terraced House in Dinghai is a residential scale volume with three interconnected, topographically responsive, successively elevated plinths and roofs. The building is flanked by distinctive gable wall forms that enclose the central courtyard. The façade is composed of three horizontal layers from bottom to top: a concrete base of horizontal formwork, a vertical wall of short-waved corrugated metal panels and large areas of glass, and glued wood beams. Upon entering, the walls open in various directions and at different heights, bringing the mountain landscape into the interior to obtain a view and light that changes over time. The three rooms are interlinked, creating a spatial transparency both horizontally and vertically and an expansion of the rooms. The wooden roof frame is carried by longitudinal steel beams, while the flat roof, which appears partially, accommodates the air-conditioning equipment and forms the rhythm of the top. The steel columns in the middle room suggest the direction of the sea on the scale of the human body.

a Main space of the second floor
b Roof hierarchy
c Exploded axonometric view
d Look to courtyard from third floor
e Master plan
f Aerial view
g Partial roof
h Stairs from second to third floor

c

d

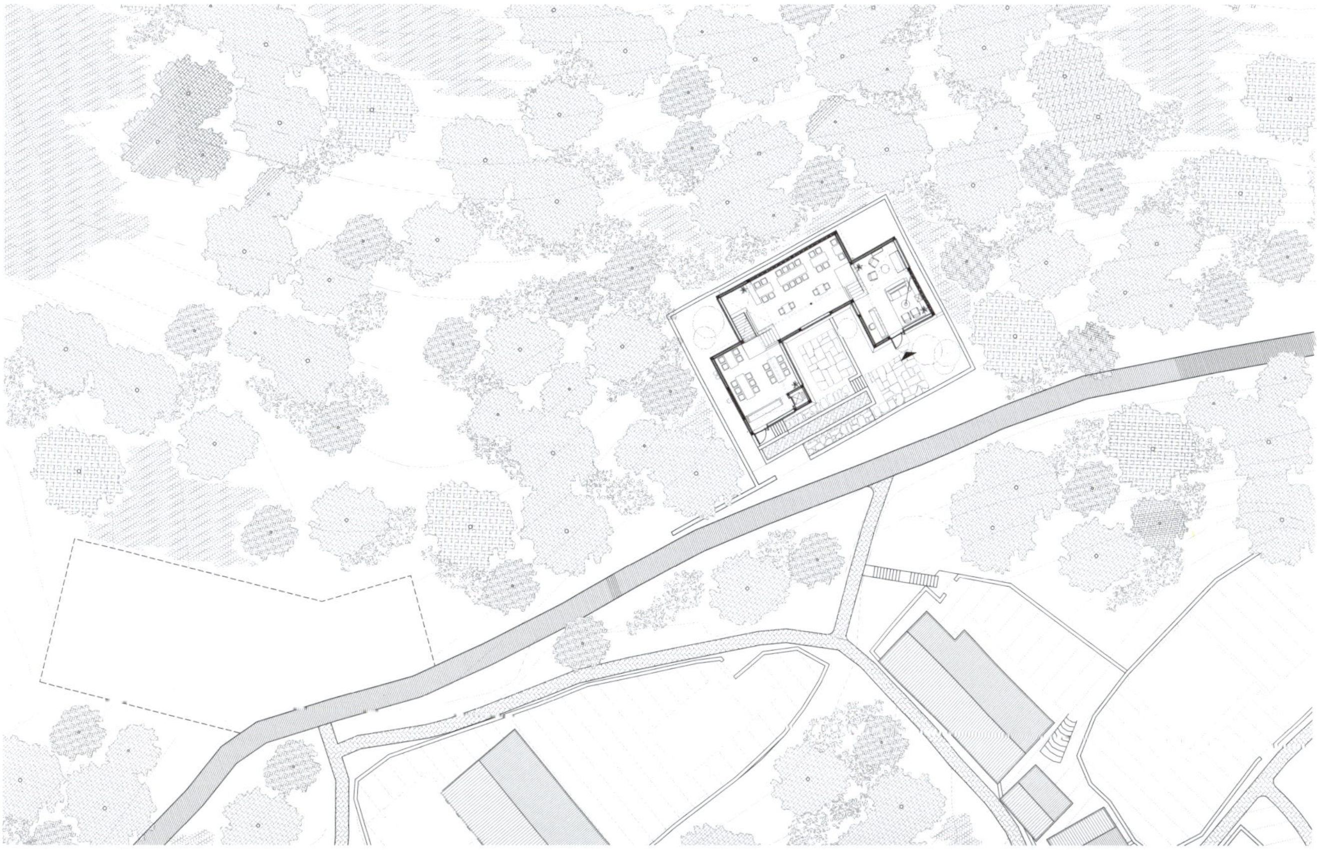

e

f g

h

March Design

Wang Tao

a **Coolette Boutique**
Location
Qingdao
Completion 2015

b **Humble House Hotel**
Location
Qingdao
Completion 2015

c **Tsingtao 1903 Bar**
Location
Qingdao
Completion 2014

March Design is a crossover design office, founded in 2006 by Wang Tao, born in 1980. It offers services in the aspects of for example small and medium architecture, landscape, spacial solutions, product, graphic and animation designs as well as installation, sculpture and other creations in the field of pure art and art collection. March Design cooperates with many professionals, which establishes a vigorous office. The works of the studio are based on two special qualities: first the creative philosophy, containing different backgrounds of designers which provides more possibilities for multidimensional ways of thinking, second, March Design keeps in mind simple and direct human demands for all their works, adapting projects to the lifestyle and way of living of each individual client. The studio takes humanism as an inspiration focusing on the being in life.

a

b

c

Location
Shaxi Old Town, Dali,
Yunnan, China
Building type residential
Completion 2018
Client Wang Tao
Gross floor area 240 m²

Wang Tao House

a

b

Architect Wang Tao built his own house as a personal space with the wish of forming a home filled with light and life. Therefore it was designed colorful and with big window façades offering views on the beautiful countryside surrounding the construction. Modern looking staircases connect the different levels and create an open spacial atmosphere. Natural materials such as wood and stone were used for the construction and also as furniture. This leads to a continuous theme throughout the whole building and brings a closeness to nature inside the house and the owner's and visitor's mind. With its simple and clean forms and the contrasts of black steel and light wood the house has become a place of quiet and the same time relaxing elegance. The project manages to combine modern design with the idea of a welcoming and cozy home connected to its surrounding nature.

a View on landscape
b Staircases
c View through glass façade
d Inside the living area
e Kitchen with modern design
f Terrace with view on countryside
g Staircase construction plan
h Floor sketches

c d

e

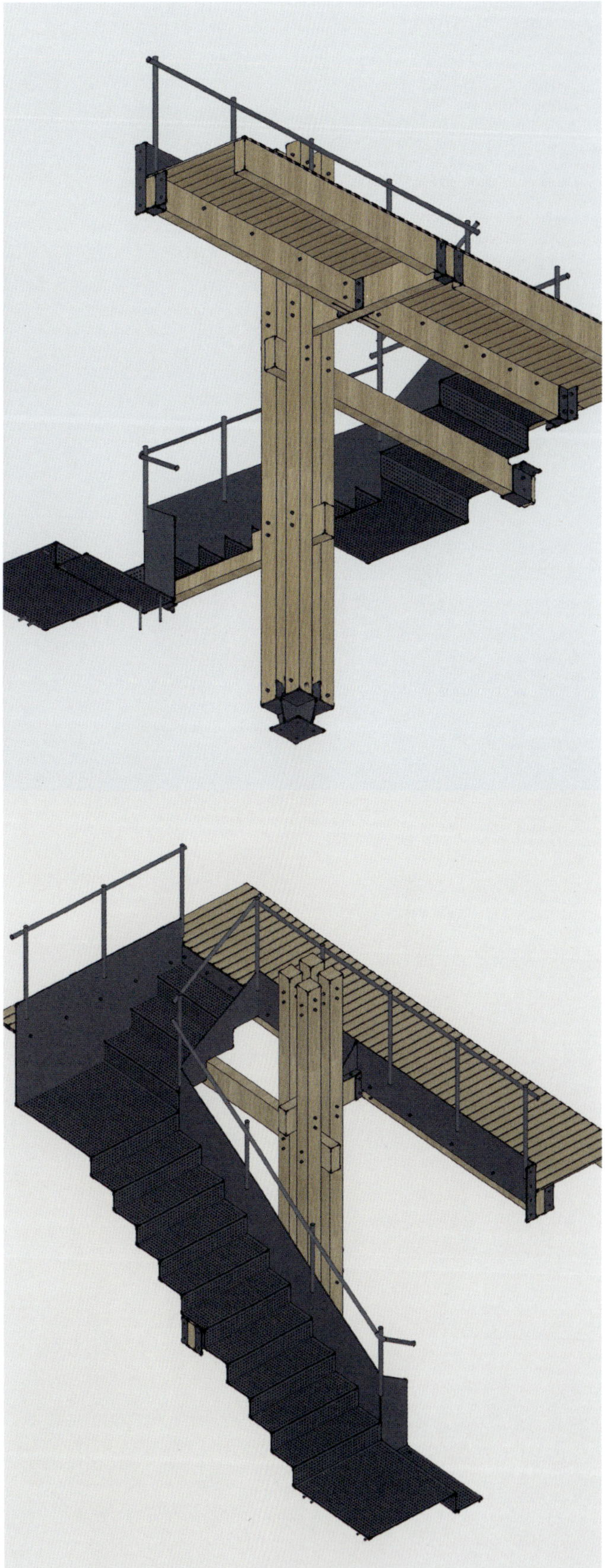

f g

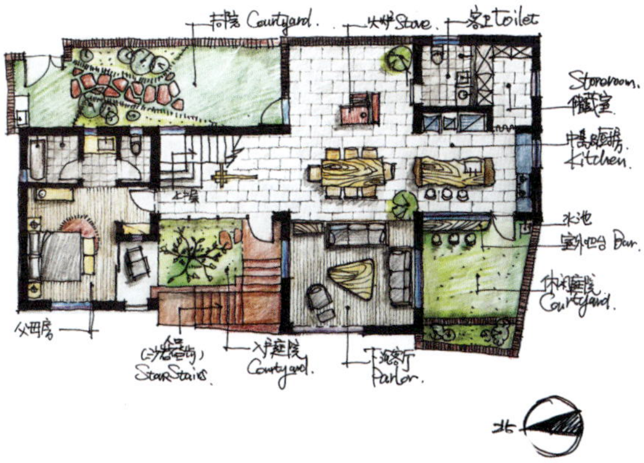
Courtyard
toilet
Storeroom
Kitchen
Bar
Courtyard
Parlor

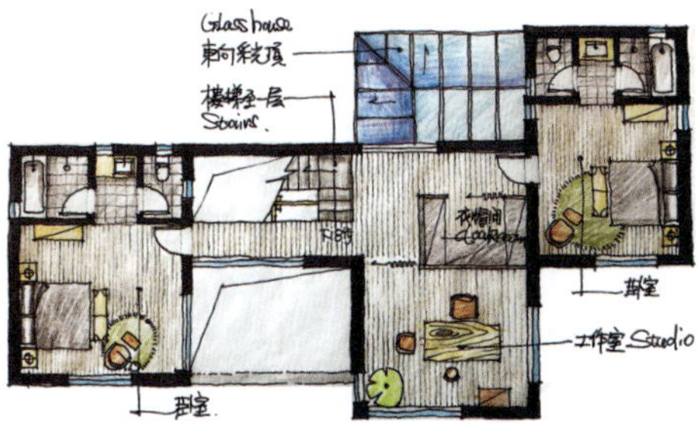
Glass house
Stairs
Studio

h

Challenge Design

Jie Li

a **Yuanlu Community Center**
Location
Chongqing
Completion 2018

b **Yulin Art Center**
Location
Chongqing
Completion 2019

c **Park Legend Kindergarten**
Location
Chengdu
Completion 2019

d **Chongqing Paradise Walk**
Location
Chongqing
Completion 2017

Challenge Design is a Class A architectural design office which was established in 2013 by Jie Li. He was born in 1974. The aim of the office has been to provide refined design and professional service since its foundation. Challenge Design has been working to find a way for realization of harmonious coexistence between architecture, human being and nature, hoping to find a possible way for bringing renewed sense experience and creating new thoughts and spatial forms through creative thinking. The company has won many international awards, including International Design Awards Architect Design of the Year, A' Design Award- Platinum Awards, and International Wood Design Awards.

a

b

c

d

Langtin Yuanzhu Experience Hall

Location
N288 Taizi Lake North Road, Wuhan, China
Building type culture
Completion 2018
Client Yuzhou Properties - Hubei Branch
Gross floor area 1,403.1 m²

a

b

This floating building, through shaping of different spaces, goes against the traditional pattern and creates a rhombus-shaped structure bringing about impressive visual impact. Based on harmonious unity of art and function, the architect created a brand new lifestyle experience hall. With 270 degree landscape vision, the building enjoys ultimate view. The sceneries, paths, squares and steps are scattered along the footway to create an ultimate overall visual, auditory experience. For the landscape architecture, Shuishi Design was hired. The presence of water blurs the inner and outer boundaries of the building, allowing it to fully integrate with the environment. This building has a series of experiential function areas such as the café, the children's activity area, the multifunction hall, the book bar and the Virtual Reality-experience room. All these functions make the space fully utilized and sustainable. The form of functional layout can reflect the continuity in space. People in this building can feel the visual delight brought out by the spatial design and immerse themselves in it. Responsible for the interior design was Dongjun International Design Consulting. The exquisite sculptures at the lobby offer ubiquitous modern stylishness and elegance. The matching of materials and the tuning of the lighting colors both contribute to a shiny effect. When people walk up the stairs step by step, natural light spills into the indoor exhibition space through a large glass window, making the exterior view unobstructed.

a 270-degree view of landscape
b Form follows function
c Square aluminum tubes
d Line of light strips
e Cross section
f Master plan
g First floor plan

c

d

e

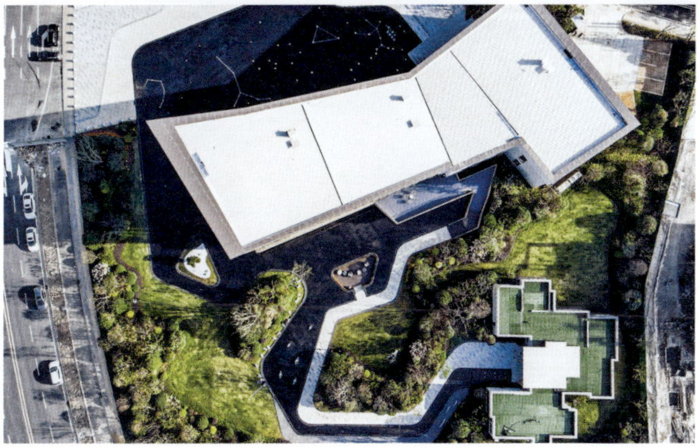

f

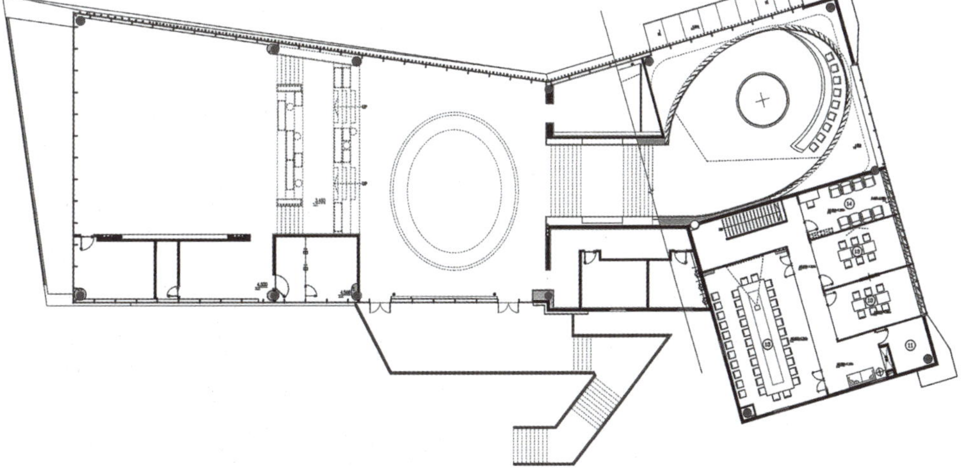

g

AT Design

Mo Shen

a Visaya Hostel
Location
Huzhou
Completion 2019

b Visaya Hostel
Location
Huzhou
Completion 2019

c Beijing House
Location
Beijing
Completion 2020

d Beijing House
Location
Beijing
Completion 2020

e Beijing House
Location
Beijing
Completion 2020

AT Design was founded in Hangzhou in early 2014 by Mo Shen, born in 1983. The core idea of AT Design is the symbiosis of heterogeneous culture, of man and technology, the symbiosis of internal and external, as well as of man and nature. The developments of the office melt cutting-edge creative design with symbiotic thinking and ecological design systems to create a pleasant and comfortable experience space. The company develops a diversified creative industry business, establishes its own complete market system orientation, firmly grasps the most cutting-edge market information, and at the same time it provides the best solutions for customers through a huge resource base.

a

b

c

d

e

Laiyee Hostel

Location
Middle Village of Liaoyuan Village, Moganshan Town, China
Building type hospitality
Completion 2019
Client Zongfeng Hu
Gross floor area 600 m²

a

b

The Laiyee B&B Hostel, with brand design by Spiritlake in the beautiful scenery of Mogan Mountain was designed according to the concept of a tree in the water. On the other hand the architectural design techniques were inspired by the five major elements of the international-renowned architect Le Corbusier: free planes, free elevations, horizontal windows, overhead columns and roof gardens. Like trees are growing free in the forest the liberation of the floor plans is used to achieve a free composed space. Technically this was made possible because of a steel structure and wooden walls. The sunken yard as semi-public space in the hall is surrounded by water features and provides a bar, where guests can meet. People can gather on the surprising staircases as well. The guest rooms take the idea of being in a tree even further providing views to the landscape. In the top-level room, the walls are painted with artistic paint to simulate the texture of the rocks in the cave and a geometric sky-light opens up to the blue sky and white clouds. The choice of materials and the way of interspersing the structure makes the building pure and independent in the environment, eliminating any deeper impact on the surrounding environment.

a Interior staircase
b Top-level guest room
c Exterior staircase
d Guest room
e Ground floor
f Combination of volumes

c

d

e

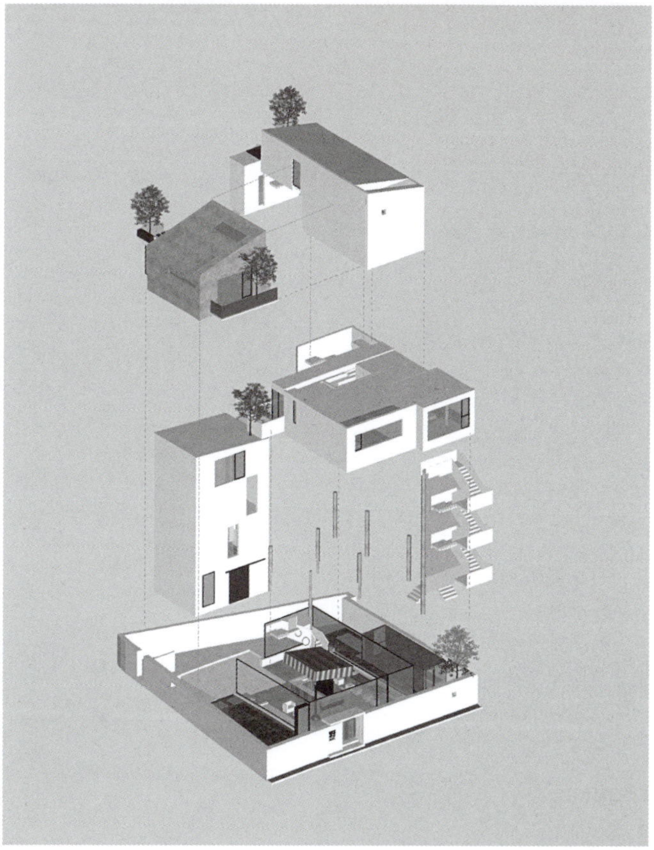

f

ZJJZ

Yu-Ying Tsai, Xuanru Chen

Sean Shen

a **Treewow Hotel**
Location
Xinyu
Completion 2020

b **Woodhouse Hotel**
Location
Zunyi
Completion 2018

c **Mountain Restaurant & Bar**
Location
Zunyi
Completion 2018

ZJJZ was established in 2017 by Yu-Ying Tsai, born in 1985, Sean Shen, born in 1986, and Xuanru Chen, born in 1986. The name of the office is 休/耕 in Chinese. The first character means rest, while the second signifies farming. When put together, the phrase means allowing land to become fallow in order to restore its fertility. The most important value for the architects is joy of design, the mission they have chosen as architects, and the desire to remain sensitive to the world. 休/耕 accordingly reminds to slow down: Fallowing is a crucial part of farming, so time can be used to lay the foundations for best works. Professional areas of expertise encompass cultural and public projects such as art galleries, libraries, museums and hotels. A guiding principal is that architecture is not limited to a physical structure that merely satisfies functions, but is also a container of space that users interact closely with.

a

b

c

Dafa Canal Tourist Information Center

Location
Tuanjie Village, Zunyi, Guizhou, China
Building type culture
Completion 2018
Client Guizhou Dafa Tourism Development
Gross floor area 3,280 m²

a

b

The Dafa Canal Tourist Information Center of Tuanjie is one of the first projects of a new government policy to alleviate rural poverty by introducing agritourism. The building is expected to become a new centerpiece for the village, boosting further development in the area. It combines offices and exhibition programs under a tiered, public roof that blends and merges into the surrounding landscape. The roof serves as a new platform for public life. Nestled in the steep mountain landscape, the building sits on a natural platform with a ten-meter drop in elevation. The stepped form results from the linked constraints of location, access, and view. The stepped façade, clad in local stone, emerges directly from the landscape in form and material, humanizing the scale of the building and working directly with the topography of the site. Viewed from below, the building appears as a composition of smaller volumes that harmonize with the surrounding nature and village. The steps become a stage for the public with a background of mountains, clouds and trees. A floating canopy of wooden tiles serves as a connection of the entrance plaza and the lobby with a semi-outdoor space inviting people to linger. Two staircases connect the different levels. One connects the meeting and office spaces, and the other serves as a gallery, creating a continuous exhibition space that leads visitors to an outdoor public terrace.

a Drop-off square
b Façade close-up
c Platform on the roof
d Ground floor plan
e First floor underground plan
f Second floor underground plan
g Side view on the tourist center
h Office
i Exhibition

c

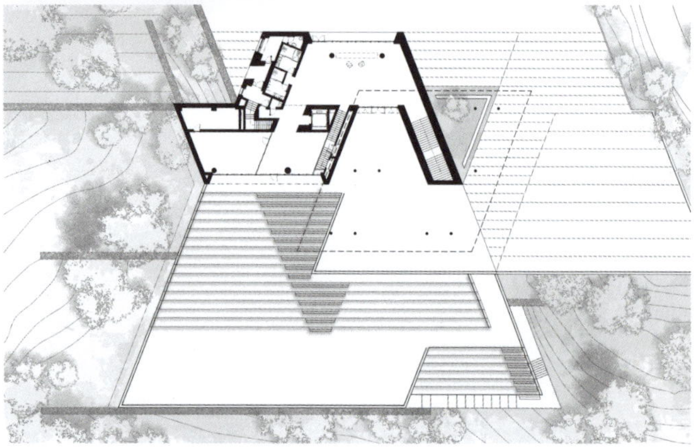

d

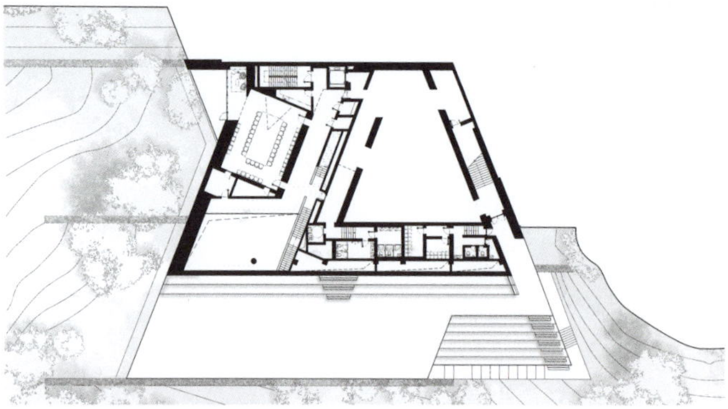

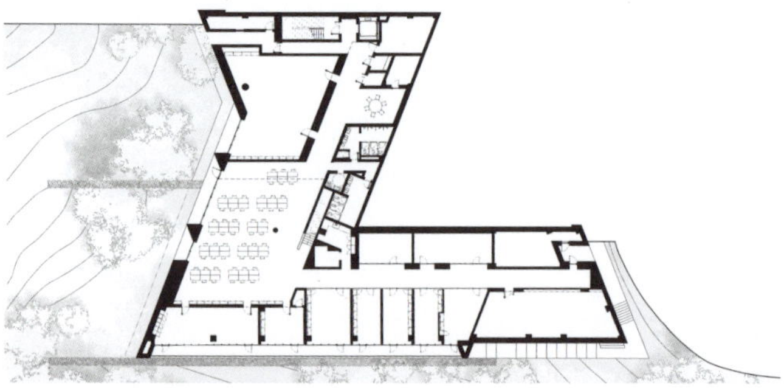

e f

g

h i

MenJue Architects

Manjun Huang

Tingting He

Fei Liu

a **Cheeweekg Kindergarten**
Location
Taizhou
Completion 2019

b **Wakened Memory**
Location
Chizou
Completion 2019

c **Zhongsen Baby Infant Growth Center**
Location
Jia xing
Completion 2019

MenJue Architects are a group of young people with attention on design innovation. In 2019, Manjun Huang, born in 1991, Fei Liu, born in 1982, and Tingting He, born in 1990, registered MenJue Architects Company in Shanghai. In project design, they start from the overall vision with design method. The focus lies on the quality of space, to approach the space itself from the physical space, creating a general language to drag everybody to the same original point of consideration, just like the growth of a tree. The principle of the office is that there is no architecture or space that could live without site. Every space has a character and this character can make one feel the existence of physical space. According to the studio architecture needs a precise action to respond the condition provided by the site, to make space, atmosphere and form perceptible.

a

b

c

Shadow of Space Baishuiquan Tea House

Location
Far East Hongxin Plaza, Pudong New Area, Shanghai, China
Building type hospitality
Completion 2020
Client Far East Hongxin Plaza
Gross floor area 500 m²

a

b

The project site is located on the ground floor of the main building. The outdoor light is filtered secondarily by the corridor to soften the internal light on the other side of the corridor space. The function of the original architectural design failed to meet the new requirements. The ground floor of the main building is nearly five meters high, which is in contradiction to the building's function. The functions of a tea house are just as important as the need for clarity in construction. In order to achieve the spatial characteristics of a tea house, it is also necessary to complete the spatial form precisely by organization. The existing space has been developed into a specific experience of place and space, and now offers a whole new way of drinking tea. This experience is based on the perimeter spatial form of the house. In the enclosing form, the top of the slope emphasizes the protection of the room. Within the circumferential form a lot of space for the tea room has been created, including the stone tea room space, the bending tea room space, the tea table and the tea room space along stairs and windows. Thus, the interior was given an external naturalness, which led to the mobilization of space: The architects let the users experience both internal and external spaces while drinking tea, but also intermediate states and entirely individual feelings of space.

a Dining room
b Dining room
c Entrance area
d House in house
e Floor and roof construction plan
f Ground floor plan
g House in house detail
h Living room
i Ground floor

c d

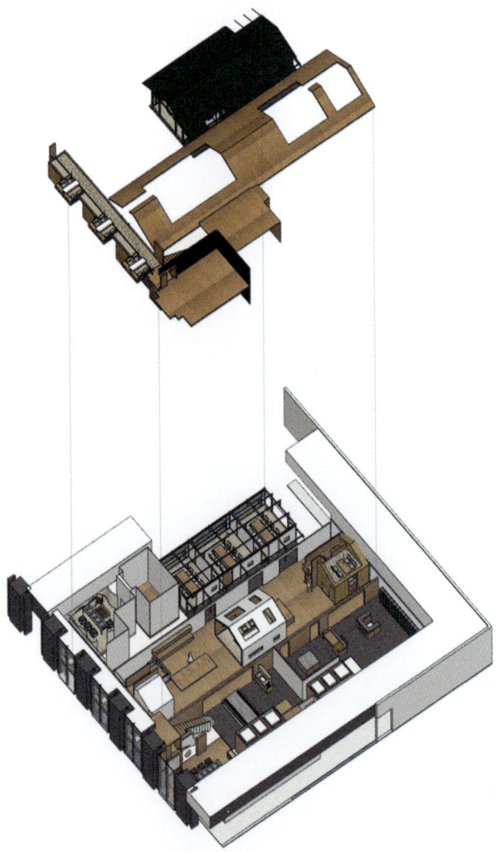

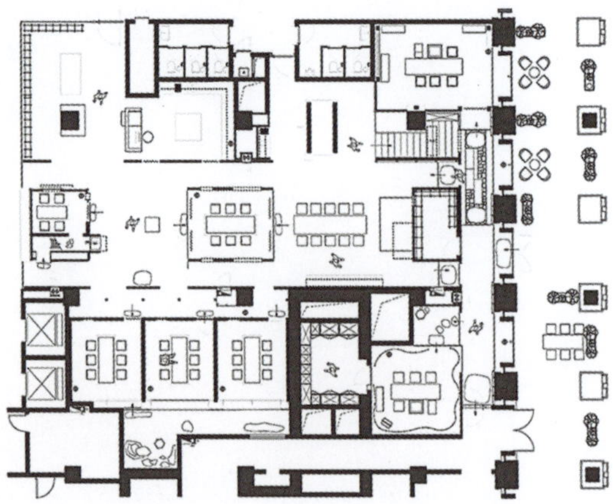

e f

g h

i

Zhang Hua Studio

Hua Zhang

a **Liuzhou Suiseki Hall**
Location
Liuzhou, Guangxi
Completion 2012

b **Jixian National Geological Museum**
Location
Tianjin
Completion 2008

c **Millet Vinegar Museum**
Location
Zibo
Completion 2018

d **Wu Qing Mission and Education Center**
Location
Tianjin
Completion ongoing

Zhang Hua Studio was founded in 2007 by Hua Zhang, born in 1956, and is linked to the Tianjin University Research Institute of Architectural Design and Urban Planning. Hua Zhang has been engaged in architectural design for more than 46 years. He provides innovative design and theory in cultural architecture, educational architecture and other aspects. His designs have won various awards for example from the Ministry of Construction or the Ministry of Education in China and also abroad for dozens of times. The studio is committed to original architecture, research direction for modern architecture fractal theory, topology theory and computer parametric design.

a

b

c

d

Yu Qingcheng Gallery

Location
18 Yingbin Road, Jizhou District, Tianjin, China
Building type culture
Completion 2016
Client Tianjin Guangcheng Investment Group Limited Liability Company
Gross floor area 1,682.91 m²

a

b

This project is full of movement and has two or more different forms at the different ends. The form is not a result but a continuous flowing and changing of physical space, a process from static to dynamic and of temporal spatial evolution, a non-focus building, a geometrical composition from linear to nonlinear changes with both topology and fractal characteristics. The whole project plays with the idea of merging contrasts into each other instead of keeping them apart. The physical space of this gallery contains ten changes including for example level-blocks developing from large to small, colors from dark to light, physical texture changing from thick to thin and two-dimensional flowing to three-dimensional space. The construction was created out of burned purple sand soil which is widely spread in the area. It is surrounded by a beautiful landscape and also contains green planting areas on its own roof.

a Wall detail
b Curved wall
c View on façade and landscape
d Stairs at the outer façade
e First floor plan
f Ground floor plan
g Interior wall design

c

d

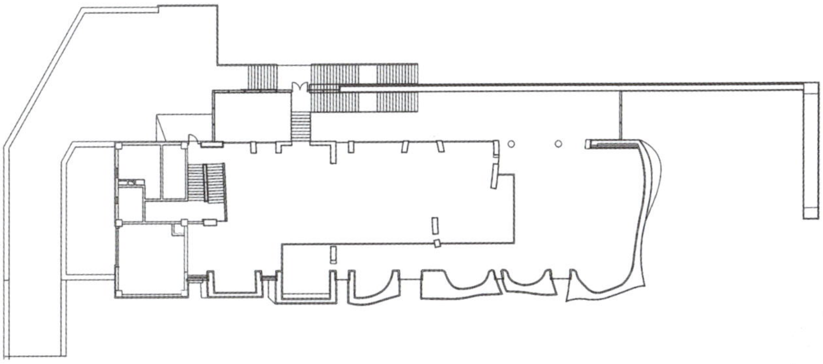

e

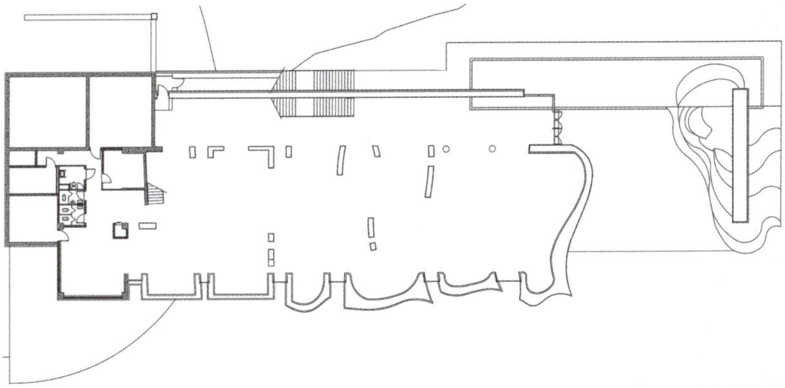

f

g

Atelier L+

Linxue Li

a **Chongming Athletic Training Center**
Location
Shanghai
Completion 2019

b **Hangzhou Civic Center**
Location
Hangzhou
Completion 2015

c **Memorial to the Body and Organ Donors**
Location
Zunyi
Completion 2020

Atelier L+ was founded in 2000 by Linxue Li, born in 1970. The studio is focused on the frontier of architectural practice on the background of China's urbanization. Using critical intervention as a strategy, it rigorously engages in the advancing architectural discourse and paradigm innovation in contemporary China. Nature based system construction and responsive ontology constitute the core principles of the research and practices. As such they enable the projects to be firmly situated within specific contexts integrating elements from local climate, natural system, as well as social, cultural and historical conditions. In total, the studio has undertaken over thirty public projects, ranging from civic buildings, culture, education and sport facilities, to urban regeneration, skyscrapers and large complexes.

a

b

c

Yellow River Ecological Tourist Wharf

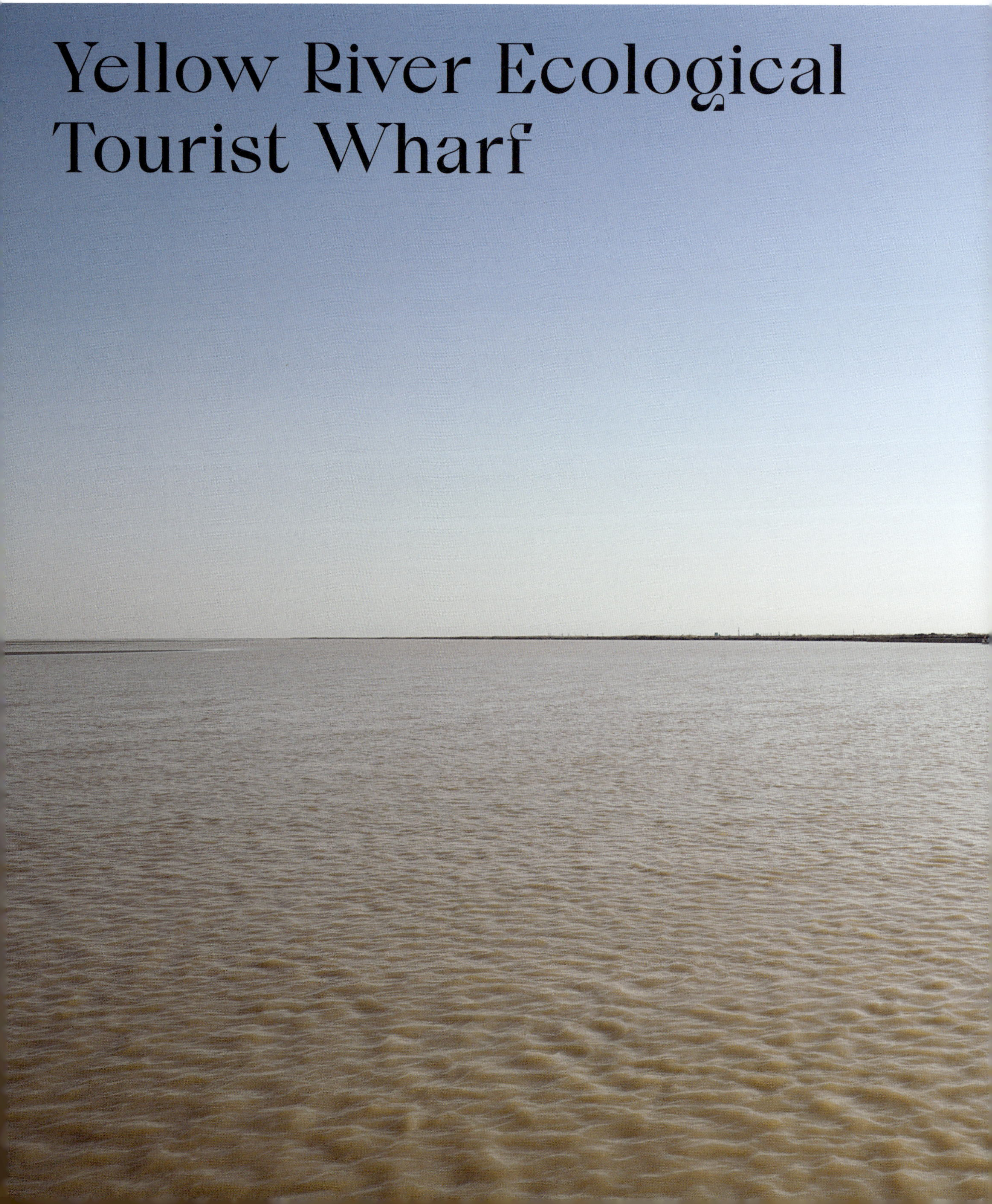

Location
Dongying, Shandong, China
Building type culture
Completion 2010
Client Dongying Tourism Development Cooperation
Gross floor area 10,000 m^2

The design and construction of the Cruise Ship Wharf of Yellow River Estuary Ecological Tourism Zone investigate architecture's intervention in nature and the relevant strategy of design. The creative integration of the program, structure, space, morphology and material is the key of the realization of architectural design. The building seeks a minimum deconstruction of the natural landscape with its floating suspension structure which integrates the structural and architectural aspects into an organic unity. As such, it has only four cores touching the ground directly. Out of concerns for sustainability, it uses hollow low-E glass and solar panels; meanwhile, the use of roof covering and insulation board achieves good insulation. The construction aims to fulfill multiple purposes: Its roof serves as an open-air theater and inside the building there is a coffee shop, a waiting hall, as well as restaurants and other private rooms. A multilayered roof deck for sightseeing was created from where visitors enjoy a wonderful view of the wetland in the surrounding area. A corridor bridge seamlessly connects the interior of the building to the wetland, creating a space for dialogue with nature.

a Floor plan
b Interior of waiting hall
c Site plan
d Tectonics of suspension system
e Night view
f Space created by suspension

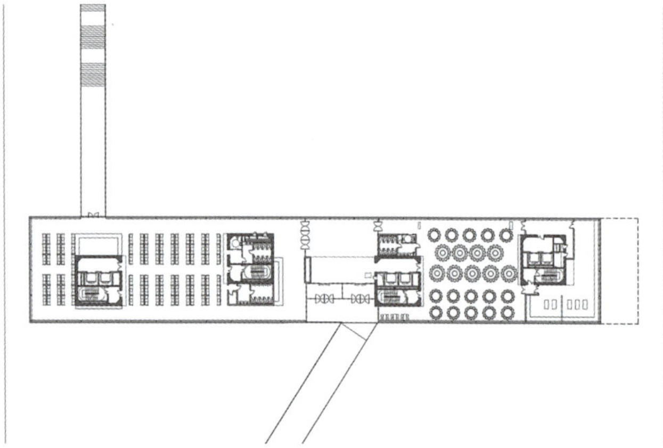

a b

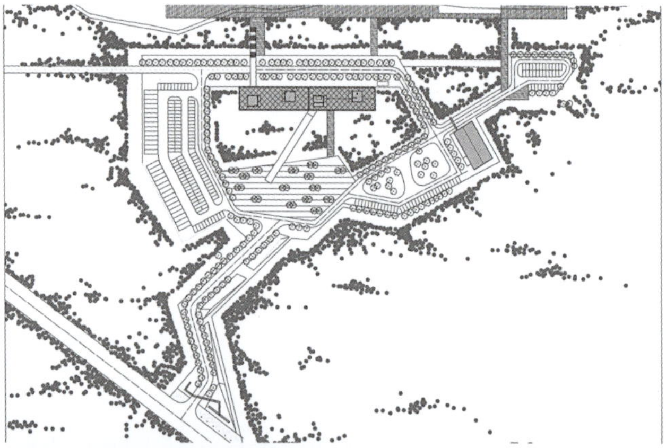

c d

e

Ida&Billy Architects

Ida Sze

Billy Chan

a **Wave**
Location
Hong Kong
Completion 2017

b **Futian Kindergarten**
Location
Shenzhen
Completion 2021

c **The Embracing Ring, Yisabu Dokdo Memorial Park Competition**
Location
Samcheok, South Korea
Completion 2018

Ida&Billy Architects is an architectural studio aimed at resolving problems and creating architectural interest out of simplicity and an integrated whole. Nature, art and humanity are the three fundamental elements of their works. The founders Ida Sze and Billy Chan have a diverse cultural background with over 20 years of working experience in Hong Kong, Beijing and Basel. The studio was established in 2013. Their first project, Bridged House, has been awarded with the Good Design Award and HKIA Annual Award. Since then they have been receiving many international design awards, including Reddot Design Award, Good Design Awards, Iconic Design Award, A' Award, DFA Design for Asia Awards and HKIA Annual Awards. In 2018, the studio was selected by Wallpaper* Magazine Architects' Directory for the 20 emerging architects from across the globe.

a

b

c

Location
5A & 7 York Road,
Kowloon Tong,
Hong Kong, China
Building type residential
Completion 2015
Client Mr. Henry Tang and
Mrs. Lisa Tang
Gross floor area 700 m²

Bridged House

a

b

The Bridged House links two existing houses of different ages and styles as one, spatially, aesthetically and spiritually, while keeping the identity of each. The landscape plinths were demolished for a generous middle garden stretching the site's depth. The swimming pool, with all enclosing walls taken down, overflows to form a backdrop for the garden. A steel bridge, connecting the houses at the second level, floats above the middle garden. This daily path of meeting, the middle garden and the pool form an overall focus. The houses' original marble cladding was stripped off and replaced with white paint and big rectangular windows. Timber parapet-tops add highlights to the neutral color. The two houses overlook each other, like neighbors in a town, and are linked up by the bridge. Stairs are expressed as a gallery of form and light. The existing structure is manipulated with new balconies and windows openings to form continuous lines or patches of forms. Tailor-made handrails emphasize touching and grabbing. Above, the skylights are designed to hide the glass frames, to blur the boundary between inside and outside. A plank fair-faced concrete slab tops the penthouse with rough texture and cement color to tie back to nature.

a Pool overflows as water screen
b New bridge over garden
c Skylight over the stairs
d Plank concrete roof in penthouse
e Sculptural staircases
f Plank concrete fence wall
g Houses overlooking each other
h Site plan
i Site section

c

d e

f g

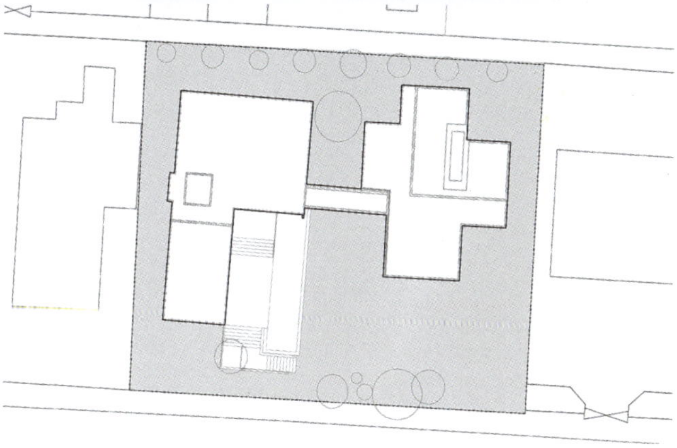

h

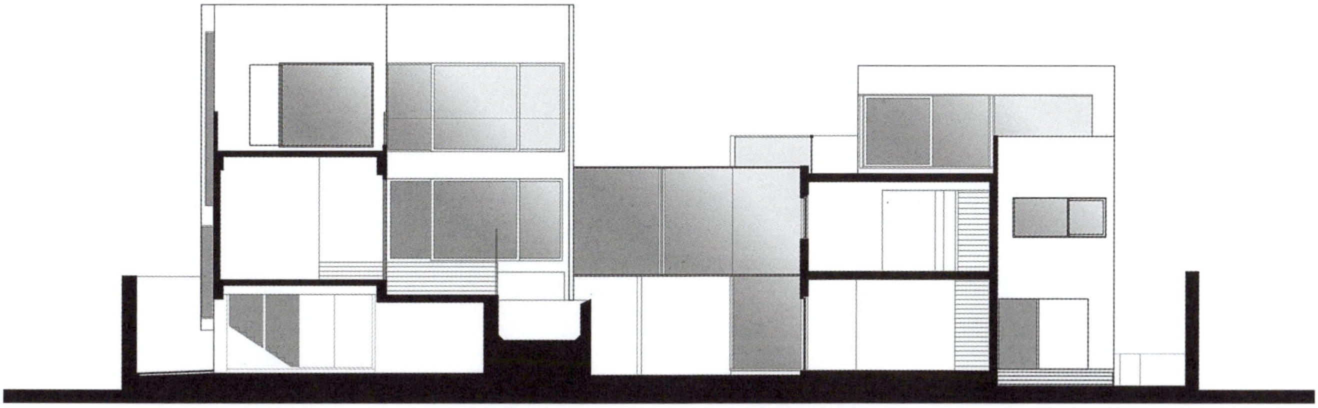

i

Nota Architects

Shiyun Qian

a **Seesaw Coffee BJ Joycity**
Location
Beijing
Completion 2018

b **Heytea Bakery Hangzhou Guoda Plaza**
Location
Hangzhou
Completion 2019

c **Lishui Two-Three House Distillery**
Location
Lishui
Completion 2018

d **HAY Wuhan**
Location
Wuhan
Completion 2019

Nota Architects is an architectural design studio founded in 2014 by Shiyun Qian, born in 1983, in Shanghai. The word Nota is taken from Latin, and refers to musical notes or annotations. Here, it stands for the perspectives or visions of the architects, who design like musicians or directors do by scripting. It's not the notes that make music, rather it's the nota in-between. The architectural design and research are based on multidisciplinary perspectives. Each project has its unique values and is promoted by adaptive thinking, consistent efforts and scientific methodologies. Nota covers design and research projects in architecture, interior design, urban environment, graphic and product design. Project types are diverse but specialize in historical building renovation, boutique hotel, cultural architecture, and supreme interiors. The office was awarded as AD100's The 100 Most Influential Architects and Interior Designers in China 2019.

a

b

c

d

Location
1F Longhutianjie Shopping Mall, 181 Tayuan Road, Huqiu District, Suzhou, China
Building type hospitality
Completion 2018
Client Seesaw Coffee
Gross floor area 235 m²

Seesaw the Garden

a

b

Suzhou, considered as Venice of the East, is well-known for meticulously designed Chinese gardens, named yuanlin in Chinese. To ensure the specialty coffee brand Seesaw Coffee an appearance for their branch that fits the region, classical Chinese gardens were aimed to be readapted and fit into a limited indoor space located in a shopping mall. Considering the art of Chinese gardens and its meaning in the contemporary context, Nota Architects created a gardening practice called zaoyuan by reinterpreting related materials, functions and garden imagery. The landscape design was realized by TT Flowers. The blue-base-terrazzo Lotus Pond (hechi) with loose sets of one table and four stools is presented in the middle. The coffee bar almost floats in the water, giving different perceptions in color as one moves around. The white-base-terrazzo, standing for white sand, fills the space between the buildings and the water. Large windows provide natural light and create depths of sceneries mixed with landscape and people. They extend the garden imagery to a greater perception.

a Panorama of the central pond
b View from the waterside pavilion
c Meeting table
d View side entrance to garden
e Morning at the side entrance
f View through glass curtain wall
g Axonometric drawing
h Ground floor plan

c

d

e

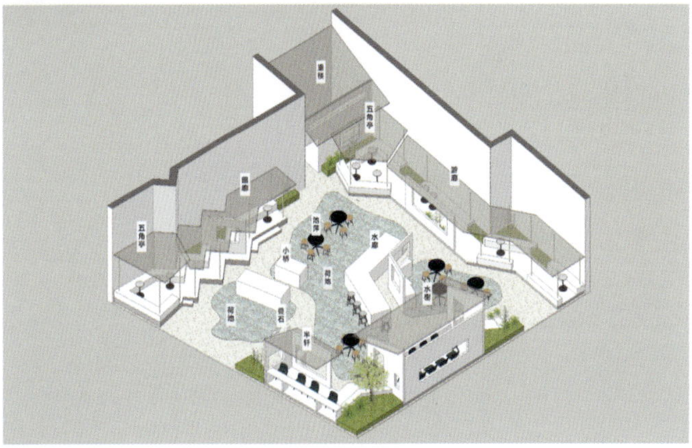

f g

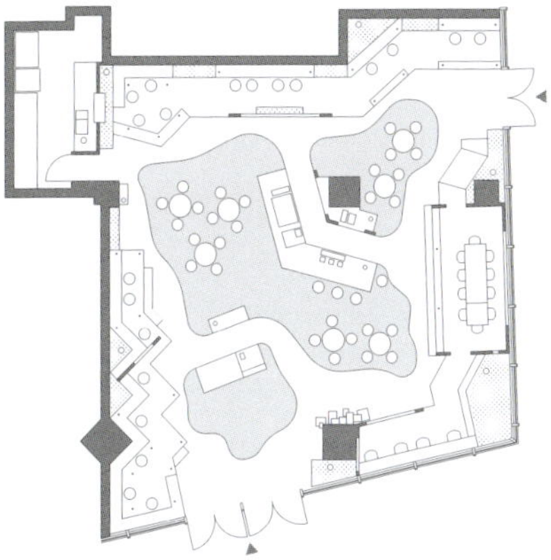

h

MAD Architects

Ma Yansong　　Dang Qun　　Yosuke Hayano

a **Absolute Towers**
Location
Mississauga, Canada
Completion 2012

b **Chaoyang Park Plaza**
Location
Beijing
Completion 2017

c **Tunnel of Light**
Location
Echigo, Japan
Completion 2018

Founded in 2004 by Ma Yansong, born in 1975, MAD Architects is being led by him together with Dang Qun, born in 1969, and Yosuke Hayano, born in 1977. The studio is committed to developing futuristic, organic and technologically advanced designs that embody a contemporary interpretation of the Eastern affinity for nature. MAD has been commissioned by clients of various backgrounds for design in urban planning, urban complex, museum, theater, social residence, old neighborhood renovation, and artworks. The office works on projects all over the globe and is successful and recognized on a wide international level. It is not only based in China, but also contains offices in the USA and Italy. Apart from architecture, MAD also focuses on design and art, participating in many exhibitions for example at the Centre Pompidou in Paris.

a

b

c

YueCheng Courtyard Kindergarten

Location

6 West Lane, Shuangqiao Street, Chaoyang District, Beijing, China

Building type education

Completion 2019

Client Yuecheng Group

Gross floor area 9,275 m²

The YueCheng Courtyard Kindergarten was built next to a senior citizens' apartment, integrating preschool education and elder care together. It was realized together with Lumia Lighting Design responsible for lighting design and Ecoland Planning and Design Corporation functioning as landscape architect. The location consisted of an original 18th century Siheyuan courtyard, an adjacent replica courtyard built in the 1990s, and a four-story modern building. MAD chose to remove the replica courtyard outside the historic 18th-century original, and replace it with a new space. This new space adopts a low and gentle posture, with a flowing motion contrasting the strict, orderly layout of the historic structure. The new design therefore finds a fitting balance between old and new. The building contains a floating roof, which forms a Martian landscape, enticing children to run and play. On the ground floor three courtyards surround several old trees of the original site, making nature a key element. These courtyard are connected to the rooftop area through stairs and slides. The interior of the building lets in sunlight through floor-to-ceiling glass walls. The transition space from the first floor to the sunken level on the east side of the lobby is cleverly designed as a theater, which doubles to a lower playground, offering space for playing and the realization of arts and sports events.

a Entrance
b Staircase and slide
c Interior axonometric view
d Bird's-eye view
e Staircase in the theater
f Play and learning area
g Ground floor plan
h Rooftop model

a

b

c d

e f

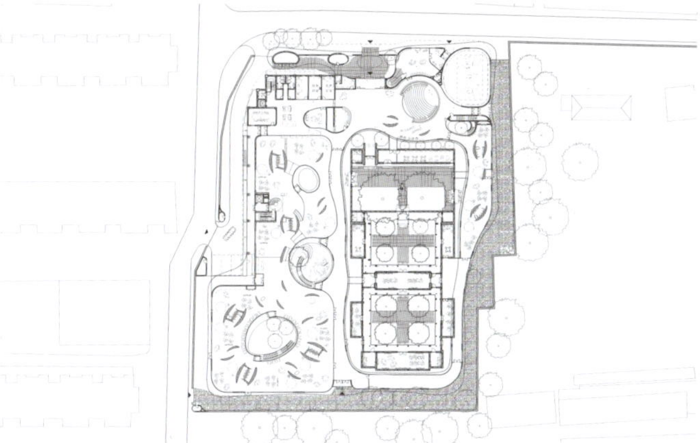

g h

Praxis d'Architecture

The studio

a **Spring Art Museum**
Location
Song Zhuang, Beijing
Completion 2015

b **Ying Gallery Renovation**
Location
Cao Chang Di, Beijing
Completion 2016

c **Max Show Center**
Location
Qing Dao
Completion 2015

d **Lake Shore Studio**
Location
Song Zhuang, Beijing
Completion 2012

Founded in 2009, Praxis d'Architecture is actively engaged in a broad range of projects of various scales, from offices, artist studios, exhibition spaces to installation and furniture. Shaohua Di, born in 1972, is the founding principal of the office. She leads the studio together with Xinxin Xu, born in 1982, Xuewei Zhang, born in 1968, and Jialin Yang, born 1994. For the studio design begins with identification and analysis of cultural and physical context of the site and drawing inspiration from it. A main focus of Praxis d'Architecture lies on the understanding that the theme of a project will be tangibly represented through the device of architecture, and determines the nature of material, light and space. The studio's projects have been widely published and received many awards not only in China but also on an international level.

a

b

c

d

Location
Zhu Yuan 2nd Street,
Airport Industrial Zone A,
Shun Yi, Beijing, China
Building type office
Completion 2018
Client Gold Concord
Gross floor area 23,607 m²

Tian Yun Industrial Office Complex

a

b

The design of the Tian Yun Industrial Office Complex was created by as a first step studying the basic office unit. The concept of modularization was applied in the design of office unit. The floor plan is defined by either one or two 8.4 meters by 8.4 meters structure frames with an additional 3.3 meters cantilever to facilitate office use. The construction is an efficient functional core that has solved the puzzle of connecting office units and maximizing the office space use to achieve a room rate at minimum 90 percent. The design of Tian Yun complex is based on the characteristic of the site. An L-shaped form was chosen from the four basic geometries to enclose the site to generate a central plaza. Each L-shaped building is made of two office units. The buildings have seven floors above ground and one basement level. The architecture façade is also based on modularization. Rounded corners emphasize fluidity and symbolize harmony in traditional Chinese culture. Curved balconies with planters surround the buildings and embrace the glazed office spaces while also creating fluid social space during work breaks. Praxis d'Architecture realized the project together with STID Group, who was responsible for interior design.

a Balcony detail
b Illuminated outer façade
c Balcony area
d Section
e Site plan
f Elevation
g Sky-lit dining hall

c

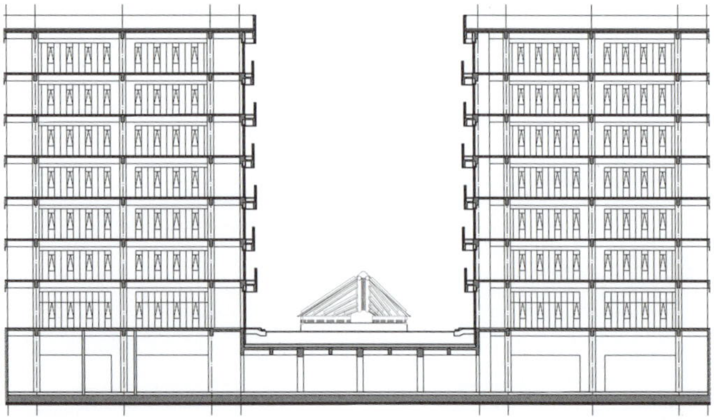

d e

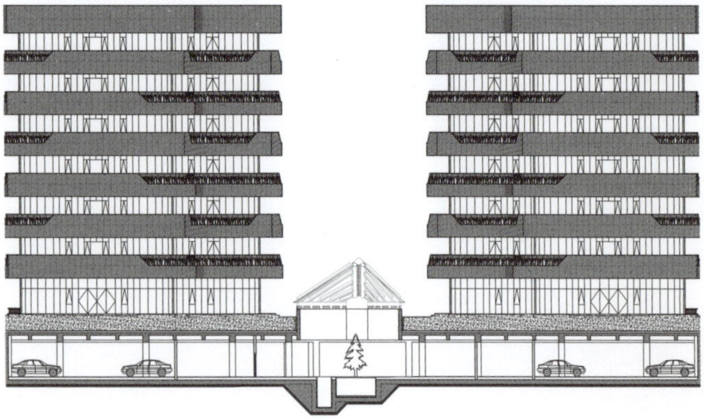

f

Hui Wang | Urbanus

Hui Wang

a Jiading "Now Factory" Creative Park
Location
Shanghai
Completion 2014

b Urban Planning Museum and Park
Location
Tangshan
Completion 2008

c Environmental Upgrade of Five Dragons Temple
Location
Ruicheng
Completion 2016

d Xihoudu Relics Ceremonial Flame Park
Location
Ruicheng
Completion 2018

Hui Wang, born in 1967, is the principal architect and co-founder of Urbanus. He is an architect licensed in New York State and a council member of the Architectural Society of China. In 1999, Hui Wang co-founded Urbanus with his partners Xiaodu Liu and Yan Meng. Based in Beijing and Shenzhen, Urbanus has become one of the most influential architectural practices in China. More than a design practice, it is also a think tank formulating architectural strategies for contemporary urbanism. Urbanus focuses on urban realities in China and seeks architectural solutions based on the researches of emerging urban problems. Its projects have received numerous prominent awards, and have been exhibited and published both nationally and internationally.

a

b

c

d

Location
Yanqing District, Beijing, China
Building type culture
Completion 2019
Client Vanke
Gross floor area 8,400 m²

Botanic Garden Expo 2019

a

b

Different from typical transparent conservatories, with the theme of the so called incredible wisdom of plants, the Botanic Garden of 2019 Beijing International Horticultural Exposition is designed as a wonderland hidden behind a mysterious veil. This concept is inspired by roots under the earth, and aims to create a kind of floating construction in the air. The building contains a functional waiting area where visitors standing in a queue are protected by the shaded area with attractive vertical roots. The spectacular project opens up a journey to experience the colorful botanic garden, showcasing the wisdom of plants' survival skills on this planet that humans can learn from. While the outer façade mainly contains colors such as different shapes of brown and gray, the inside of the building is filled with the green colors of the plants and full of light coming through the glass of the roof. The project was realized together with Office Ma responsible for landscape design and EA4 Design Department functioning as the local design institute.

a East façade
b Gray space
c Ground floor plan
d Conceptual sketch
e Exterior view of north side
f Sky footpath inside conservatory
g Inside the conservatory
h Under the sky footpath

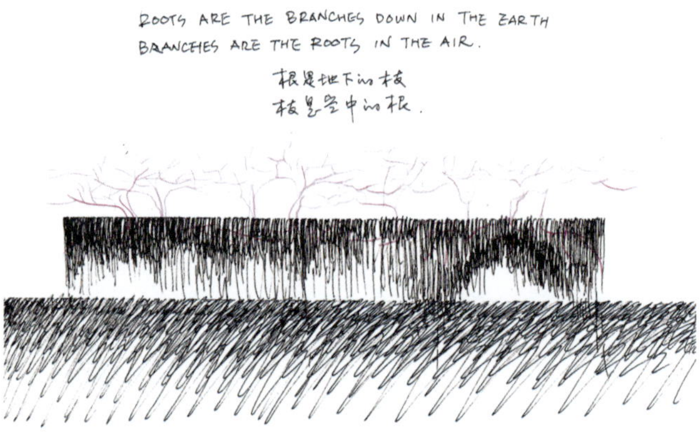

c d

e

f

g h

AZL Architects

Lei Zhang

a **Ruralation Museum Hotel**
Location
Nanjing
Completion 2020

b **Concrete Slit House**
Location
Nanjing
Completion 2007

c **BingDing Wood Kiln**
Location
Jingdezhen
Completion 2019

Professor Lei Zhang, born in 1964, founded AZL – Atelier of Zhang Lei Architects – at Nanjing in 2000. The studio has grown into an avant-garde design firm with worldwide influence, and the representativeness of contemporary Chinese architecture. Followed with the international convention, the organizing of AZL Architects is based on partnership. Under the academic leading of Lei Zhang, the studio has attracted a big amount of young talented people. AZL Architects has a total number of 111 employees of professional and assistant designers in different disciplines. Besides this around 40 graduates and interns at home and abroad participate and assist the design work. The scope of service includes schematic design and design development in architecture, interior and landscape, professional construction documents design in architecture and structure.

a

b

c

CIPEA No.4 House

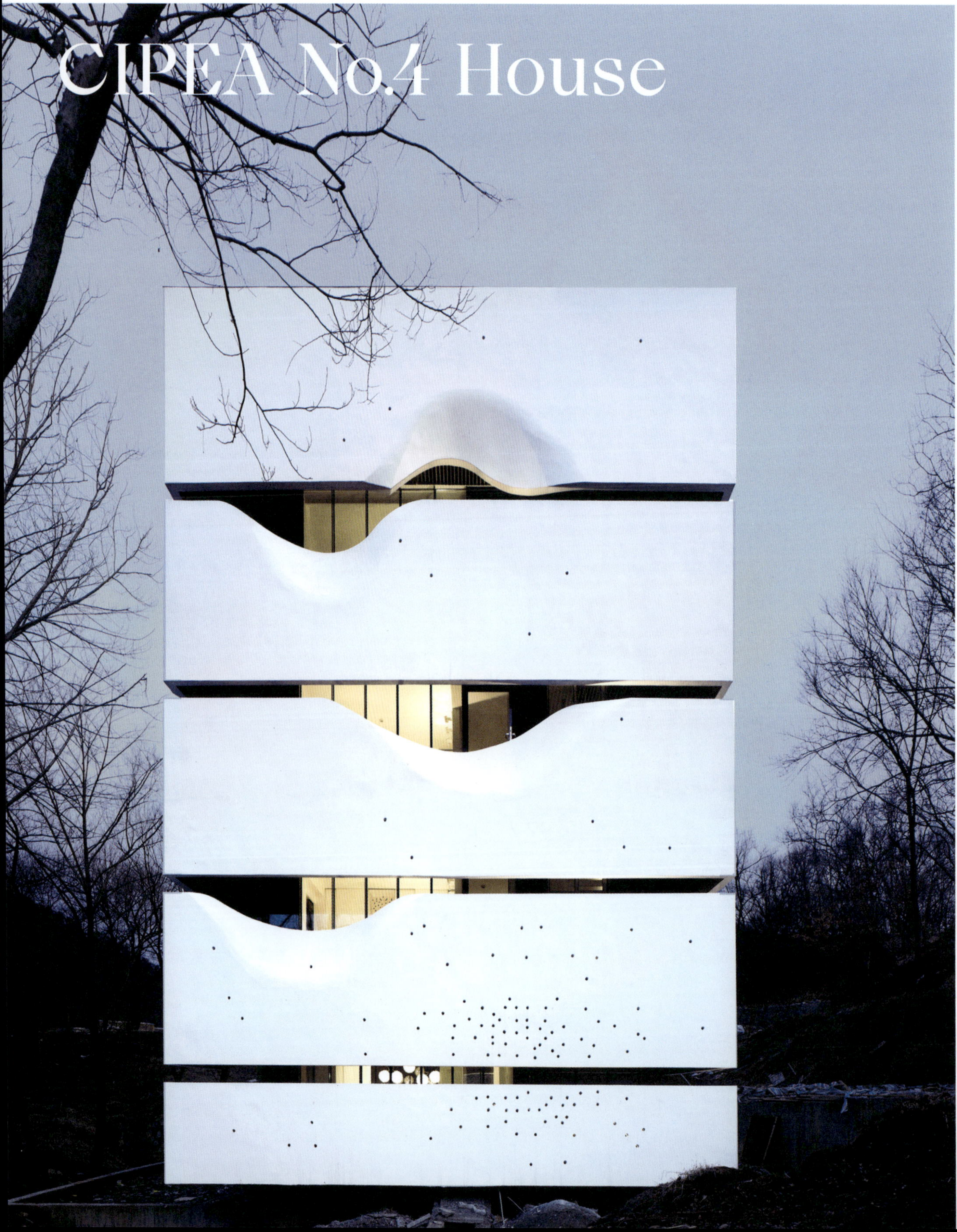

Location
Nanjing, Jiangsu, China
Building type culture
Completion 2012
Client Sifang Cultural Group
Gross floor area 500 m^2

a

b

Situated in Laoshan Forest to the West of central Nanjing city, China International Practical Exhibition of Architecture, short CIPEA, began in 2003 to bring twenty-four renowned international and domestic architects together onto one site. CIPEA consists of four public buildings and twenty small houses. In accordance with the brief, the houses should have at least five bedrooms, public spaces, and hospitality accommodations on 500 square meters. The Number Four Blockhouse sits on a particularly valley site, nestling the house into the landscape. Four cubic floors are stacked vertically, allowing for minimal site excavation and land use. The ground floor features living and dining spaces quietly enveloped in the surrounding forest and overlooking a stream while a communal roof terrace rises to just above the trees. The roof merges into the landscape as another living space, completed with a pool and wooden deck within the panorama of the forest. The geometric shape is sculpted from concrete and finished in a white protection surface. A minimal opening to the surrounding landscape is the only perforation of the richness inside the house. The horizontal break of each floor, in combination with larger unique curved apertures on each floor, frame vistas in the spirit of Chinese landscape scrolls. Prescribed views have a long tradition in Chinese art history and traditional Chinese gardens, designed to make the viewer reconsider and contemplate the landscape.

a Construction from the west
b View from forest
c Bathroom
d Living room
e First and second floor plan
f Model
g Section
h View from northwest

c

d

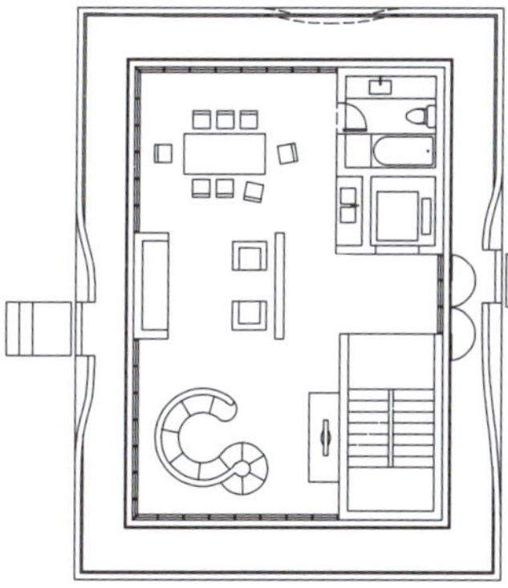

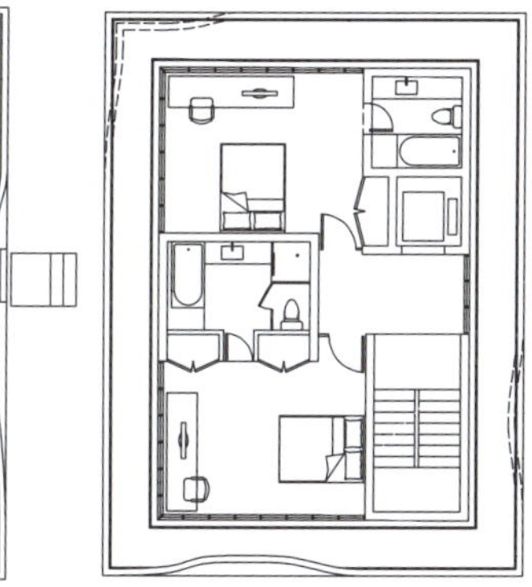

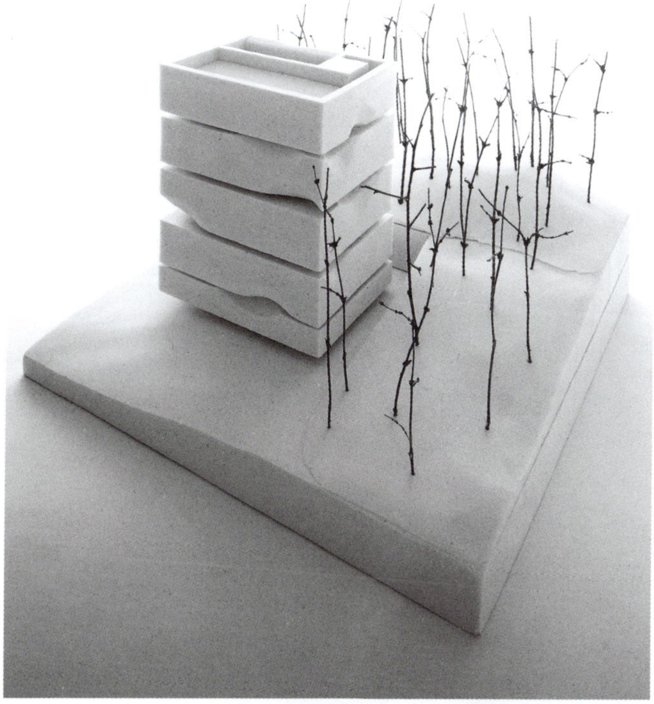

e f

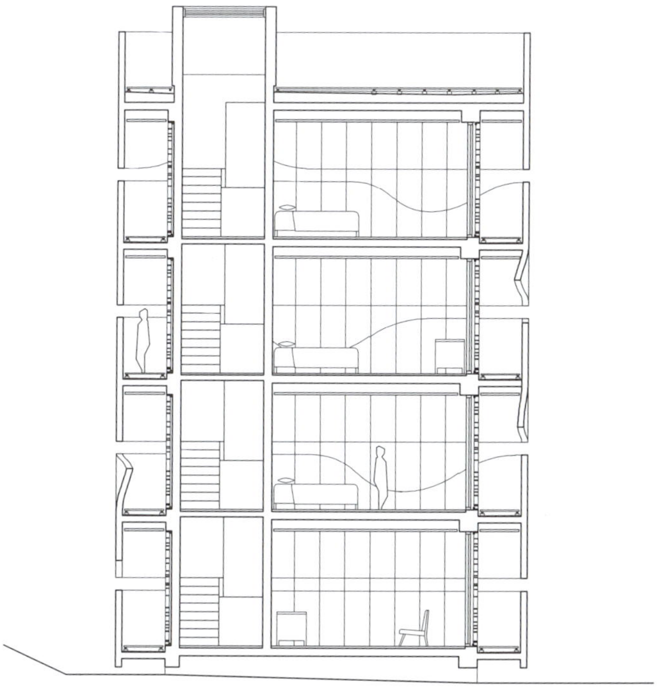

g h

Studio Zhu Pei

Pei Zhu

a Minsheng Museum of Modern Art
Location
Beijing
Completion 2015

b Yang Liping Performing Arts Center
Location
Dali, Yunnan
Completion 2020

c Shou County Culture and Art Center
Location
Anhui
Completion 2019

Studio Zhu Pei was founded in 2005 by Pei Zhu, born in 1962, who is dean, professor of CAFA School of Architecture, visiting professor of Harvard University and Columbia University, Hon. FAIA. In the last 15 years, the office has been committed to the exploration and practice of contemporary architecture, arts and culture field. An array of experimental and innovative works have been created based on the design philosophy of nature architecture. The studio is recognized for its experience concerning the ability to blend forms, space and light with great contextual sensitivity and to utilize the unique qualities of each project to create a concept-driven design. Studio Zhu Pei specializes in seamlessly integrating new projects into contexts with particular natural, cultural and historic importance.

a

b

c

Jingdezhen Imperial Kiln Museum

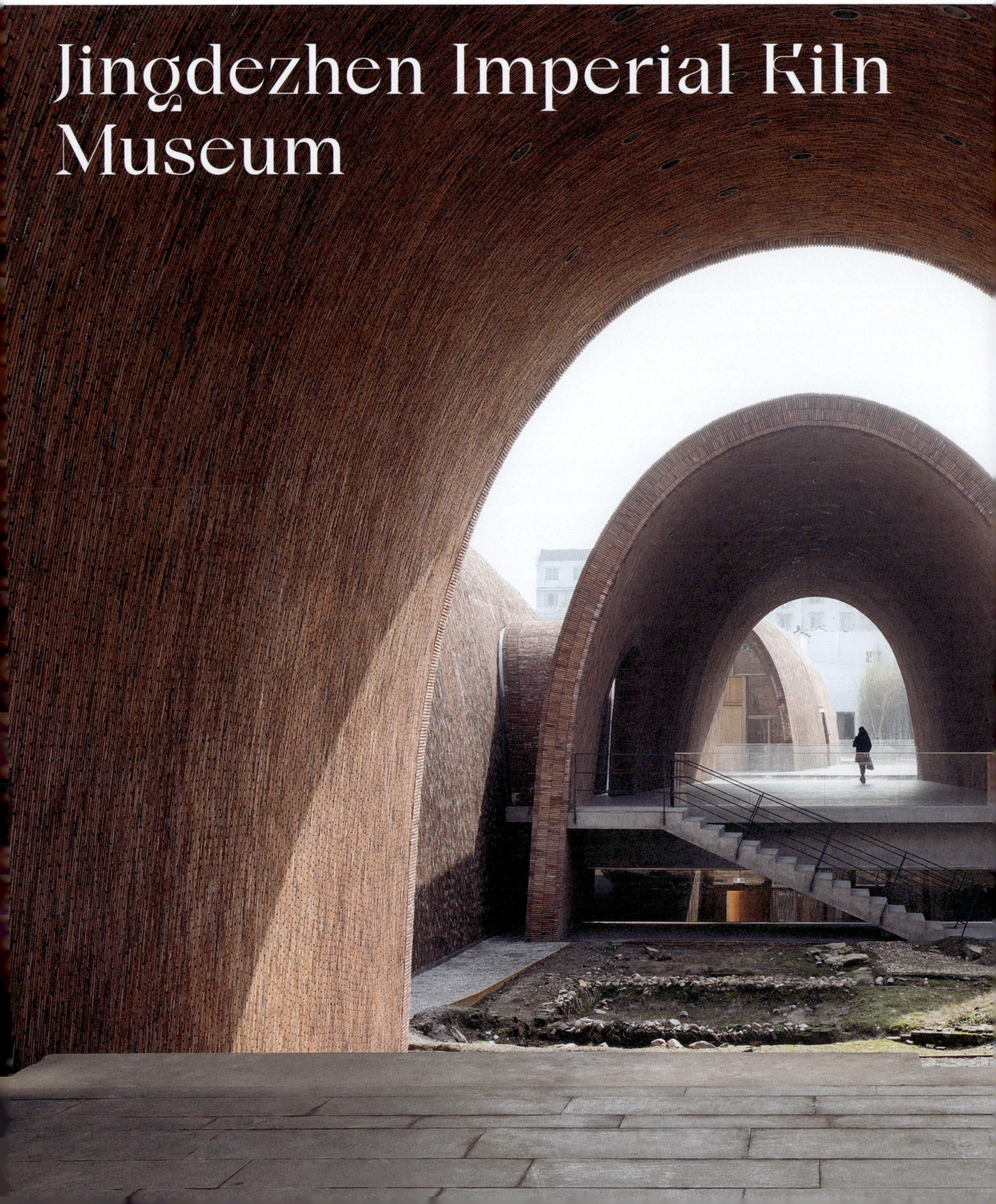

Location
East gate of Royal Kiln Factory, Jingdezhen 333000, Jiangxi, China

Building type culture

Completion 2020

Client Jingdezhen Municipal Bureau of Culture Radio Television Press Publication and Tourism, Jingdezhen Ceramic Culture Tourism Group

Gross floor area 10,370 m²

The most important Chinese porcelain manufactures of the last thousand years are located in the city of Jingdezhen. The surrounding region is known for its deposits of clay and kaolin, the raw materials for pottery in China. The remains of the porcelain industry, dating back to the Ming and Qing dynasties, surround the site of the new Imperial Kiln Museum. In order to create the museum, the studio studied this place and its history carefully, even integrating archaeological findings into the museum design. The museum comprises eight vaults based on the traditional form of the kilns. On the lower level, indoor and outdoor spaces are interconnected. Each of the vaults and courtyards, together with the first floor, form a three-dimensional space with a strong local cultural grounding. The project was realized together with the Architectural Design and Research Institute of Tsinghua University. Its arch-like ground structure connected with water basins and small bridges makes it unique and fascinating for visitors who would like to experience the local history.

a Aerial view
b Foyer
c View in between open vaults
d Auditorium
e Vault-shaped voids
f Preliminary sketch

a

b

c d

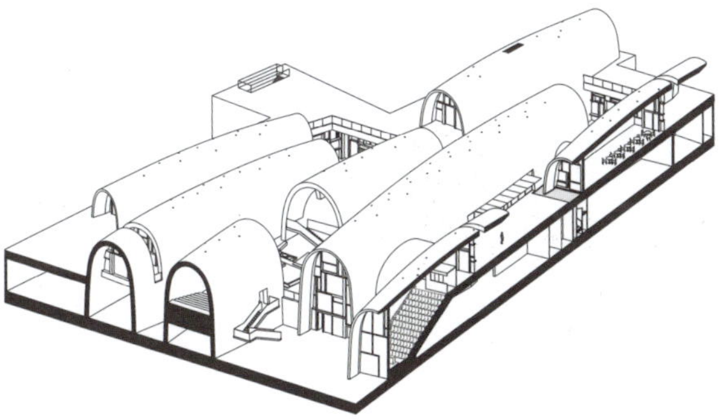

e

f

Turenscape

Kongjian Yu

a **Concert Hall**
Location
Wulinyuan, Zhangjiajie City, Hunan Province
Completion 2007

b **Stone Inscription Culture and Arts Center**
Location
Danyang City, Jiangsu Province
Completion 2011

c **Tourist Service Center**
Location
Linzhou City, Henan Province
Completion 2016

Kongjian Yu, was born in 1963, has received his Doctor of Design Degree at Harvard Graduate School of Design and won the IFLA highest honor – 2020 Sir Geoffrey Jellicoe Award in 2020. He founded Turenscape in 1998. The company is a certificated first-level design institute by the Chinese government. With over 500 professionals, Turenscape is a multidisciplinary design team that provides quality and holistic services in architectural design, landscape design, urban design, environmental design and engineering. It has planned and designed over 300 ecological cities and 1,000 landscape projects in China. Turenscape's projects have earned great international reputation for innovative and environmentally sound designs, have won 13 ASLA Professional Awards in the past ten years and five World's Best Landscape Awards at the World Architecture Festival.

a

b

c

Location
Suining County, Jiangsu, China
Building type religious
Completion 2014
Client Suining County Planning Bureau of Wetlands and Gardens
Gross floor area 40,000 m²

Moon-Floating Temple

a

b

This project is located inside the Baitang River Wetland Park in Suining and is a non-palatial modern temple complex designed with non-traditional techniques. The unique and tradition-breaking architectural form and style of the Moon-floating Temple has, since completion, become a distinctive cultural site and a place for Buddhist Zen rites to be held. Inspired by modern architecture and landscape, the architectural complex reflects ancient Zen ideas of emptiness and anatta, which describes the Buddhist believe of the nonexistence of a personal and immortal soul. The design is a modern interpretation of traditional Buddhist temples. At the same time, the design explores how the spatial language of Zen ideas can connect with ordinary people. The construction of the new temple has allowed ideas that have not changed for thousands of years to be re-explored. The Moon-Floating Temple is the first, and currently the only, modern non-palatial site for Buddhist activities in China. The layout of the entire complex is integrated and complementary to the water and garden landscapes, combining ecology and comfort, simplicity and aesthetics, Zen meditation, and mind-enriching connection to water and sky. Since opening, the temple has been well received by both Buddhists and the larger public, becoming a model for the harmonious integration of humans and ecology, religious and secular, modern and old.

a Mahavira Hall interior
b Buddhist Relic Tallinn
c Architecture details
d Mahavira Hall section view
e Moon-Floating Temple site plan
f Lotus pond

c

d

e

f

Wutopia Lab

Ting Yu, Erni Min

a **Sinan Books Poetry Store**
Location
Shanghai
Completion 2019

b **Aluminum Mountain**
Location
Huizhou
Completion 2020

c **Shrine of Whatslove**
Location
Tonglu
Completion 2018

Wutopia Lab was founded in 2013 in Shanghai by the chief architects Ting Yu, born in 1972, and Erni Min, born in 1981. It is an architecture company based on a new paradigma of believing in a complex system and that regards Shanghai's culture and lifestyle as a starting point, using architecture as a tool to promote sociological progress within building practice. Wutopia Lab is dedicated to link different aspects of urban life such as traditional, daily and cultural to interpret urban lifestyle, and to develop a contemporary Chinese aesthetic. While facing each project, Wutopia Lab's practices are promoted to show different innovative strategies, thinking modes and forms. The studio is committed to comprehensive design, not only to complete the concept of buildings and intensify them, but also focuses on early planning, analysis, landscape and interior design.

a

b

c

Eight Tenths Garden

Location
151 Jiayi Road, Shanghai, China

Building type culture

Completion 2016

Client SHI Huijuan

Gross floor area 2,000 m²

a

b

Eight Tenths Garden was originally a two-story sales center on a triangular street corner with a four-story circular hall embedded on the top. Now it serves as a multipurpose art space that boasts offices, a library, study rooms, a café, a restaurant, and chess rooms. The revitalization of the building was supposed to reveal and symbolize the life-based spirit of Shanghai. Obsessive minimalism and the creation of an exaggerated scene was prevented. The entrance is a small courtyard formed by the two sides of a triangular street wall. The natural complexity of the classically Chinese-inspired garden is an allegory for the diversity of Chinese history. The landscape design for this was realized by Atelier Vision. A winding path progresses through the garden and into the modernly simpler space which primarily houses the client's collection of Chinese enamelware. S5design was responsible for the interior design of the project. In response to the increasing international lifestyle, the building's program has also been adapted to include B&Bs in hopes of garnering greater appreciation for Chinese culture. Crucial for the design was to remain in context with the architecture of the neighboring street shops. A steel curtain was used to insulate this vibrant environment from the project. This simple architectural gesture creates the effect of a parallel reality. Visitors can easily slip behind the veil escaping from the bustle of Shanghai's cosmopolitan streets.

a Backyard
b Façade
c Bird's -eye view
d Ground floor plan
e Main hall
f Yard on second floor
g Design sketch

c

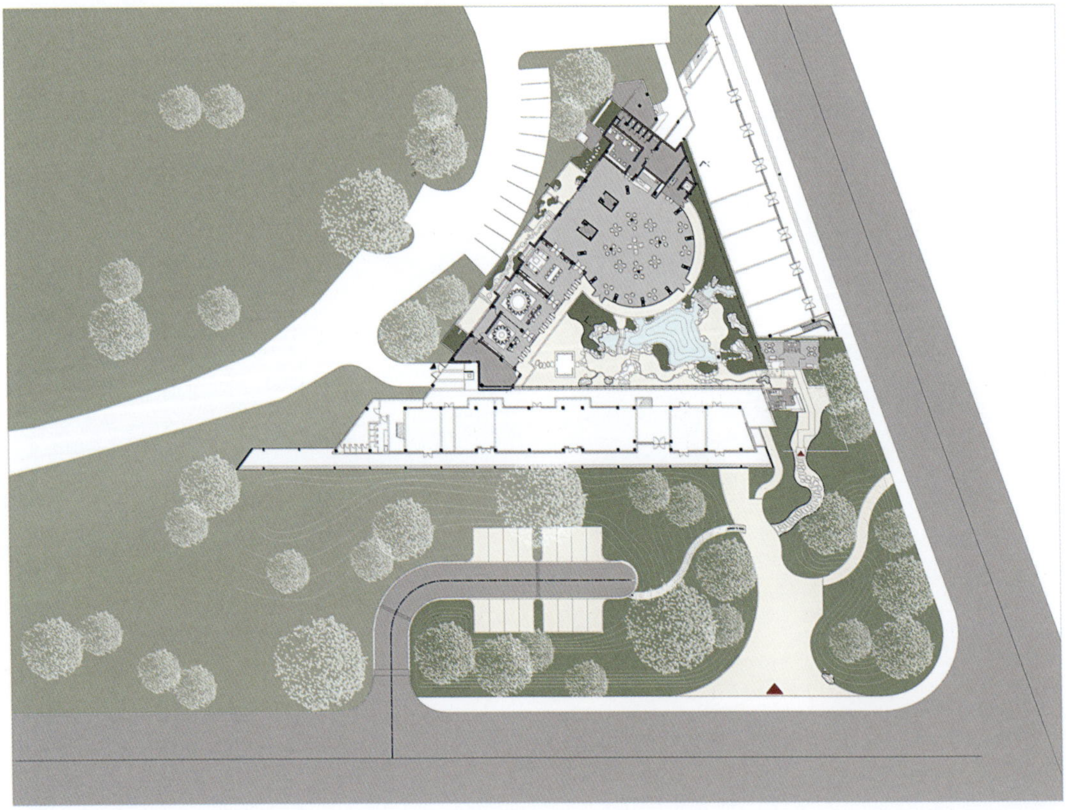

d

e f

g

Atelier Archiplein

Feng Yang, Marlène Leroux, Francis Jacquier

Fang Weiyi, Wang Mingbo

a **Beijing Hutong**
Location
Beijing
Completion 2010

b **Fox House**
Location
Félines, France
Completion 2018

c **Alpex Museum**
Location
Scionzier, France
Completion 2020

Atelier Archiplein is an architecture office of two French and three Chinese partners, founded in Shanghai in 2008 by Marlène Leroux, born in 1982, and Francis Jacquier, born in 1982. Today the studio is led together with Feng Yan, born in 1976, Fang Weiyi, born in 1980, and Wang Mingbo, born in 1980, and is based in Geneva. The practice of the office is focusing on a critical approach of urbanization phenomenon. Therefore the office claims a methodological practice based on local, cultural resources and promoting use of natural materials. Recently they have published the work "terre chinois" on the renowned Metispress edition that is analyzing the urbanization process of Chinese countryside. On the architectural side, Atelier Archiplein realizes several buildings using massive stone construction and wood, as an historical, cultural and ecological alternative.

a

b

c

Tianzhushan Tourist Infra-structure

Location
Tianzhushan Mountain, China
Building type hospitality
Completion 2011
Client confidential
Gross floor area 950 m²

a

b

Tianzhushan Tourist Infrastructure benefits from its exceptional location surrounded by the Tianzhushan Mountain. It tries to approach the philosophy of combining natural and artificial forms in a coherent and harmonious whole. The building is seen as an extension of the existing topography. It bends and follows the shape of the surrounding mountain in a flexible movement. It offers furthermore an opportunity for hikers and visitors to rest from their walks across the area around. The construction can be accessed from the first floor and includes a ramp which leads to the water level. Two types of relations with the surrounding nature are proposed through the façade which sometimes frames the landscape and sometimes offers vast openings which make the construction feel light-filled and bright. Visitors can experience a unique and exceptional view over the beautiful scenery and enjoy tea and food inside. The grayish color of the building fits the natural colors of the mountain's stone around and makes its appearance seem in harmony and union with nature. The same time it also offers clear defined shapes forming a modern-looking design.

a Connecting ramp
b Connecting ramp close-up
c Dining room
d View from terrace
e Front façade
f Scenery of the surrounding area
g Section and façade
h Ground floor plan

c

d e

f

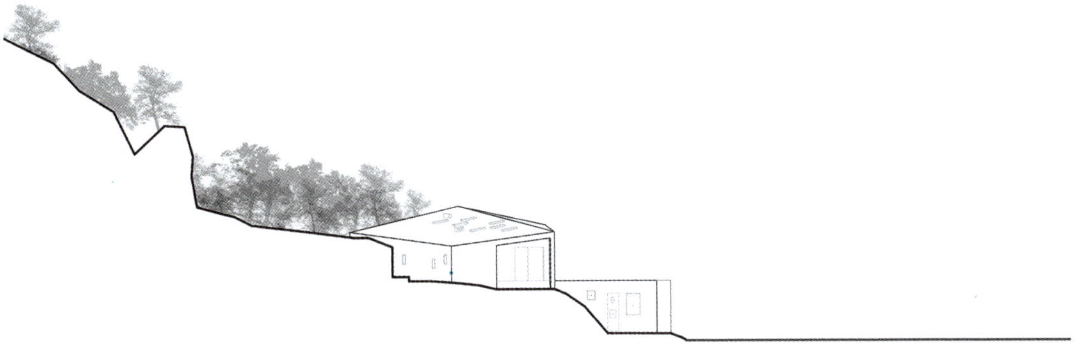

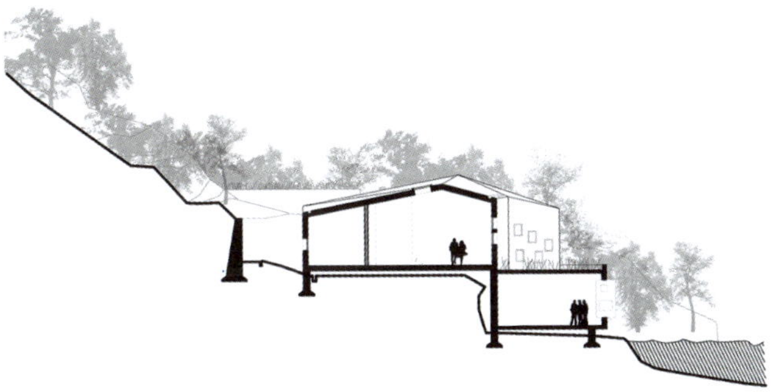

g

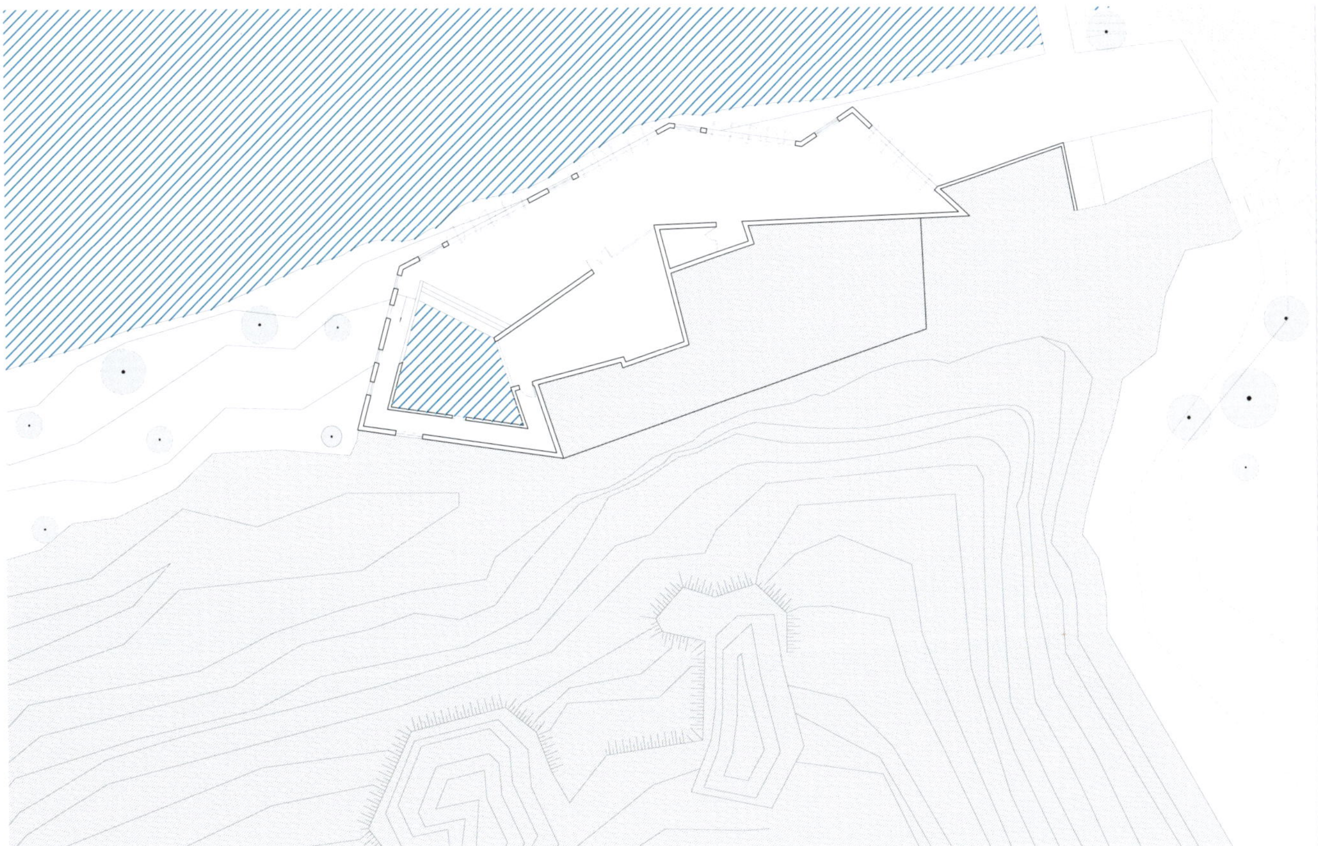

h

3

3andwich Design / He Wei Studio
Beijing
www.3andwichdesign.com
52–57

A

aoe
Beijing
www.aoe-china.com
220–225

AT Design
Hangzhou
www.atdesign.hk/china/
256–261

Atelier Alter Architects
Beijing
www.atelieraltercn.com
88–93

Atelier Archiplein
Shanghai
www.archiplein.com
340–345

Atelier DYJG
Beijing
www.dylandscape.com
142–147

Atelier L+
Shanghai
www.atelierlplus.com
280–285

Atelier XÜK
Shanghai
www.atelier-xuk.com
196–201

AZL Architects
Nanjing
www.azlarchitects.com
316–321

B

B.L.U.E. Architecture Studio
Beijing
www.b-l-u-e.net
70–75

Bao Wei Architecture Office, BWAO
Beijing
www.b-a-o.cn
28–33

Benjai Architecture
Shanghai
www.benjaicn.com
226–231

C

Challenge Design Pte Ltd.
Shanghai
www.challenge-design.com
250–255

CLOU architects
Beijing
www.clouarchitects.com
82–87

Continuation Studio
Hangzhou
www.continuation-studio.com
238–243

Coordination Asia Architecture
Shanghai
www.coordination-asia.com
22–27

Crossboundaries
Beijing
www.crossboundaries.com
94–99

CU Office
Beijing
www.cu-office.com
112–117

D

DnA_Design and Architecture
Beijing
www.designandarchitecture.net
40–45

G

Group of Architects
Hangzhou
www.goa.com.cn
160–165

H

Hallucinate Design Office
Shenzhen
www.hallucinate.com.cn
166–171

HHDFUN
Beijing
www.world-architects.com/de/hhd-fun-beijing
124–129

I

Ida&Billy Architects
Hong Kong
www.idabilly.com
286–291

Interval Architects
Shanghai
www.interval-architects.com
172–177

L

LLLab.
Shanghai
www.lllab.net
34–39

Luo Studio
Beijing
www.luostudio.cn
148–153

M

MAD Architects
Beijing
www.i-mad.com
298–303

March Design
Qingdao
www.marchdesign.cc
244–249

MenJue Architects
Shanghai
www.mj-architects.cn
268–273

Miao Design Studio
Shanghai
www.pumiao.net
154–159

MTMdesign
Shanghai
www.mtmdesign.co
136–141

N

Neri&Hu Design and Research Office
Shanghai
www.neriandhu.com
208–213

Nota Architects
Shanghai
www.notaarchitects.com
292–297

O

O&O Studio
Hong Kong
www.oandostudio.com
214–219

P

People's Architecture Office
Beijing
www.peoples-architecture.com
46–51

Praxis d'Architecture
Beijing
www.praxisdarch.com
304–309

R

RhineScheme
Beijing
www.rhinescheme.com
232–237

RooMoo Design
Shanghai
www.roomoo.cn
58–63

S

Scenic Architecture Office
Shanghai
www.scenicarchitecture.com
130–135

Shing & Partners Design Group
Guangzhou
www.spdg.hk
76–81

Sò Studio
Shanghai
www.sooostudio.com
100–105

Superimpose Architecture
Hong Kong
www.superimposearchitecture.com
118–123

SWA Group
Shanghai
www.swagroup.com
202–207

T

Taolei Architectural Design Co, Ltd.
Beijing
www.i-taoa.com
64–69

Temp
Beijing
www.te-mp.org
178–183

Turenscape
Beijing
www.turenscape.com
328–333

U

U10 Atelier CADG (United Design 10 of China Architecture Design & Research Group)
Beijing
www.10atelier.com
106–111

Urbanus
Beijing
www.urbanus.com.cn
310–315

W

Hui Wang
Beijing
www.urbanus.com.cn
310–315

Wutopia Lab
Shanghai
www.wutopialab.com
334–339

Y

Yuan Ye Architects
Beijing
www.yuanye-architects.com
190–195

Z

Zhang Hua Studio, Tianjin University Research Institute of Architectural Design and Urban Planning Co., Ltd.
Tiamjin
www.aatu.com.cn
274–279

Studio Zhu Pei
Beijing
www.studiozhupei.com
322–327

ZJJZ
Shanghai
www.zjjz-atelier.com
262–267

ZZHK Architects
Chengdu
www.zzhk-archi.com
184–189

3andwich Design
52

Wu Ang
269 c

Tom Arban
299 a

Arch-Exist
251 b, 59 c, b, 60, 61, 62 d, 63, 83 c, 185 b, 186–189, 35 b, 303 d

Diego Arenas
136 top

Atelier Alter Architects
89 a, b, c, e, 91 b, 92 c, 93

Atelier Archiplein
340

Atelier XÜK
196, 197 a

AZL
321 f

Iwan Baan
317 b

Jing Bai
275 d

B.L.U.E. Architecture Studio
70

Benjai Architecture
226, 228, 229, 230 d, 231

Wiebke Beyer&LLLab.
34

Lv Bo
191 a, b

BWAO
28–33

Javier Callejas
168–171

Baiqiang Cao
311 d

Hao Chen
198, 199 a, 200, 201 e, g, 210–213

Nina Chen
22

Su Chen
275 a, 276, 277, 278 c, 279

Vanessa Chen
233 b

Continuation Studio
238, 239 a, c,

COORDINATION ASIA
23–27

Creat AR Images
303 h, 334–339, front cover

Cubicform Xiao
136 bottom

Yuhao Ding
101 a, b, c

Peter Dixie & LOTAN Photography
35 c

DnA_Design and Architecture
40

Zhuopeng Du
250, 251 d

Duocai Photograph
126, 127 a

Léo Fabrizio
341 b

Tian Fangfang
302 a, 303 f

Liang Feng
110 c

Shuanxian Feng
304

Shuxian Feng
305 c, 307 b, 309 g

Dmitry Fironov / Wikimedia Commons CC-0
16

Shen Fuzhi
193 b, 194 c, d, f

Christian Gahl
233 a

Zhi Geng
173 a, b, c, 174–177

Laurian Ghinitoiu
265 a

gilad / Wikimedia Commons CC-By 2.0
17

Lei Go
112

GOA
160 top, 161 a

Mark Goodwin / Archmospheres
119 a, b, d, e

Fernando Guerra | FG+SG
36, 37 a, b, 38 c, 39 e, f, h

Lian He
306, 307 a, 308 c

Frédéric Henriques
342–346

Highlite Images
89 d, 90, 92 d

Yiyun Hou, Wang Tao
246–249

Ligang Huang
221 a, b, c, 222–225

Hufton+Crow
299 b, 300, 302 b, 303 e.

Ida&Billy Architects
287–291

Liu Jia
184

Jiesu
191 d

Weiqi Jin
47 c, 53–57, 91 a, 113, 149 a, c, 150–153, 179–183

Shi Jinzhong
230 c

Eiichi Kano
71 c, 72–75

Zhang Ke
185 c

Shuilong Lang
160 bottom, 161 b

Tao Lei
64–69

Chan Li
145 a

Shan Liang
293 a, 131 d

Yi Liang
94

Banye Lin
82 bottom

Qing Lin
146

Ke Liu
108, 109

LLLab.
35 a, 38 d, 39 g

David Lloyd
203 a, b, c

Lujing Image
251 c

Hengzhong Lv
161 c

MAD Architects
298

Nianshu Mao
310

March Design
244

Derryck Menere
137 a, b, d, 138–141

Pu Miao
154–159

Cheng Ming
269 a, b, 270–273

Mirko, Beijing Shardis-land Technology Co
120–123

Modern Lady
292

Motch
268

N/A
148

Nacasa & Partners
299 c

Thomas Ng
286

O&O Studio
219 g, h, i

Hiroyuki Oki
137 b

Panshiyi
118

Pedro Pegenaute
209

People's Architecture Office
46, 47 b, 51 e

Brando Posocco
114–117

Aurelien Poulat
341 c

Prism Image
251 a.

Project-Icon
119 c

Wei Qi
316

Shiyun Qian
293 c

Zhang Qingling
76 bottom, 77–81

RhineScheme Beijing
236 d.

Qiu Ripei
227 a, b, c

RS Beijing
232

Scenic Architecture Office
130

Schran Image (Shengliang Su)
161 d, 162, 163 a, b, 164 d, e

Schran Image
323 c, 324–327

Théophile Serig
341 a

Huang Shangwan
149 b.

Michael Shiu
76 top

Shuhe
83 b

ShuHe Photography Beijing
233 c, 234, 235, 236 c., 237

Silkroad, Beijing
233 d

Jonnu Singleton
203 d, 204–207

Sò Studio
100, 105 e, f

Jim Stephenson
167 a

Studio Zhu Pei
322, 323 b

Shengliang Su
131 a, b, c, 132–135, 197 c, 281 a, b, 311 a

Guodong Sun
143 c, d, 144, 145 c, 147

Yijia Sun
280

Xuguo Tang
199 b, 201 f

Wang Tao
245

Bill Tatham
202

Fang Fang Tian
215 b, 216, 217, 218 d, 219 e, f, 263 a

Tim
58

Tokyo SS Architectural Photography Co., Ltd.
282–285

Turenscape
328, 330–333

U10 Atelier
CADG
106

Chris van Uffelen
18

Larry Wen
220

Hongbin Wan
102–104, 105 h

Gen Wang
143 b

Pengfei Wang
293 b., 294–297

Wenliang Wang
166, 167 b, c

Xiangrong Wang
143 a

Zhenfei Wang
124, 125, 127 b, 128, 129

Jianquan Wu
221 d

Qingshan Wu
83 a, 84–87, 96–99

Alila Wuzhen
164 c, f

www.pxfuel.com/en/free-photo-ovozr / Wikimedia Commons CC-0 1.0
20–21

Zhi Xia
95 a, 240, 241 a., b, 242 d, 243 f, g, h, 314 e, 315 f, g

Hao Xu
293 d

Yifei Xu
197 b

Cao Yang
191 c

Chaoying Yang
95 d, 311 b, c, 312, 313, 315 h

Chaoying Yang, Lenz Wong
95 b, c

Jiaxi Yang & Zhe Zhu
208

YANJU Studio
172

Hongefei Yao
142

Li Yao
317 a,c, 318–320, 321 h

Katt Chung Yap
215 a, c, 218 c

Song Ye
256–261

Wei Yidong / Zhao Hongfei
227 d.

Haiwei Yu
107 b, 111 g

Kongjian Yu
329

Weimin Yu
252–255

YUAN Visual Studio
190

Ye Yuan
192, 193 a, 194 e, back cover

Yuchu
82 top

Zhao Yun
178

YUUUUNSTUDIO
59 a, 62 c

Changheng Zhan
48–50, 51 f

Daxin Zhang
274

Guangyuan Zhang
107 a, c, 110 d, 111 e, f

Hua Zhang
275 b, c., 278 d

Zhangyu Architecture Photography
281 c

Yilong Zhao
239 b

Liang Zheng
88

Fang Zhenning
323 a

Xia Zhi
71 a, b, d, 305 a, b

Ruogu Zhou
305 d.

Shifan Zhou
145 b

Rui Zhu
47 a

Wang Ziling
41–45

ZJJZ
262, 263 b, c, 264, 265 b, 266, 267

ZZHK Architects
185 a, d

Imprint

The Deutsche Nationalbibliothek lists this publication in the Deutsche Nationalbibliografie; detailed bibliographic data are available on the Internet at http://dnb.dnb.de.

ISBN 978-3-03768-267-8

www.braun-publishing.ch

1st edition 2021

Editor Editorial Office van Uffelen
Editorial staff and layout Lara Wörner
Graphic concept Eva Finkbeiner
Reproduction Bild1Druck GmbH, Berlin